Russian novelist, I  to be obtained not by it all that is not gold. Duncan makes the c in the Word of God, and shows that all the accretions to truth that are offered by tradition, human philosophy, self-interest, liberalism, and other factors must be carefully washed away. Only then can we know the truth that sets us free. I commend the writer for his pointed and fact-based presentation of this vital theme.

—*Mark L. Williams, D.D.*
General Overseer, Church of God
Cleveland, TN

Isaiah the prophet warned of a day when "truth would stumble in the streets" (see 59:14). Similarly, Pastor Bobby Duncan has sounded a cry that must be heard by the church today. The very title of this book puts forth a question that will pierce your spirit and help validate your commitment as a witness of Jesus: *Is Truth Enough?* In a day of market-driven compromise where dollars dominate most decisions, the very core question some are asking in ministry today is, "Can I afford to be true to the truth?" Pastor Bobby Duncan addresses this crucial issue with studied and focused precision. His facts are accurate. His thesis is sound. His passion is evident. Most importantly, the question is answered. Read it and you'll see.

—*Tim Hill, D.D.*
General Director, Church of God World Missions
Cleveland, TN

I highly recommend *Is Truth Enough?* to every pastor, teacher, and youth leader to utilize in ministering to those they serve. In these end times, Satan is doing everything he can to distort the truth of God's Word and rob God's children of the daily bread they need for victorious living.

—*Ron Martin*
Administrative Bishop, Great Lakes Region
Chicago, IL

Bobby Duncan has exposed the post-Christian culture for what it really is—a culture without *the truth*—and laments that the modern church has contributed to the demise of biblical truth by turning to a message of self-sufficiency, commercialism, and human philosophy in a quest for self-fulfillment. Every true follower of Christ who reads this book will be challenged to turn to God's Word . . . and allow it to be the guide for living in a world that has turned from biblical principles. *Is Truth Enough?* should be read by every church leader, pastor, and Bible school student.

—*Dennis Tanner*
Administrative Bishop, Church of God Scotland
Glasgow, Scotland

We tend to appreciate the thoughts of people who express ideas that agree with our own—thoughts that underscore our correctness and build up our egos. However, it is a far more difficult task to hear a warning from a seer—warnings often dismissed as irrelevant, out of date, or simply too harsh. The

Bible expresses the value and accountability of a watchman on the wall, and in this book, the author has fulfilled the command of Ezekiel 3:17 to "give them warning from Me." Bobby Duncan is seeing in the realm of the Spirit and is giving a warning from God at a very critical time. . . . The body of Christ is facing its stiffest challenge in what seems to be the eve of the coming of the Lord. Our society is rushing headlong toward destruction. The message of the Church must be clear and Christ-centered. Nothing but the supernatural move of God through His Church and His members will accomplish His work. That which has begun in the Spirit cannot be perfected in the flesh. The carnal man cannot guide us through these times. May God help us to pause and consider the warning lest we join the crowd to destruction!

—*James A. Jones*
Pastor, Southern Hills Church of God
Oklahoma City, OK

Is Truth Enough? comes from the heart of a man I know very well and strikes a resounding chord to all who will hear. It will challenge every believer to wisely guard the truth revealed in Jesus Christ.

—*Scott Duncan*
Pastor, Repurpose Church
Brunswick, OH

IS TRUTH ENOUGH?

IS
TRUTH
ENOUGH?

"Buy the truth, and do not sell it."
PROVERBS 23:23

BOBBY G. DUNCAN

PATHWAY PRESS

Managing Editor: Lance Colkmire
Editorial Assistant: Tammy Hatfield
Copy Editor: Esther Metaxas
Technical Design: Gale Ard
Cover Design: Michael McDonald

ISBN: 978-1-59684-785-9

❧❧

Table of Contents

Dedication

To every servant of God who freely publishes the truth
as it is revealed in our Savior Jesus Christ.

❧❦

Foreword

In *Is Truth Enough?*, Bobby G. Duncan has put his finger on the pulse of today's culture and how it has penetrated the church. Examining tradition, human philosophy, self-interest, personal promotion, marketing techniques, creative thinking, religious education, and legislation, he offers a unique perspective on how each of these areas has impacted the church. Using current business terminology that encourages leaders to "look outside the box" in meeting today's challenges, Duncan suggests that maybe the church has adopted that philosophy with regard to truth—that perhaps some are spending too much time looking outside the box, that is, outside the Bible, to find solutions that can only be found inside the Bible. He presents a clarion call to carefully consider where we are today in regard to truth, and to make the adjustments necessary to again capture the sound, solid principles of God's Word and to walk therein.

The message of this book is richly illustrated. Drawing from personal experience and historical events, Duncan presents an interesting, readable account that holds your attention and makes you anticipate what is coming next. The illustrations add a clarity that makes the truths shared here come alive with meaning and application.

The facts in *Is Truth Enough?* are thoroughly researched, drawing from scientific evidence, broad-based studies, and historical documents. To these, add sound biblical interpretation and you have a compelling case for the truth. Fair-minded readers will find it difficult to refute any of the arguments made in support of truth. Believers will find confirmation for the truths they hold so dearly.

Duncan writes out of deep conviction that obviously comes from the heart. Concerned about what he sees as a turning away from sound doctrine and turning to nice-sounding platitudes, he calls the reader back to the basics of the Bible. *Is Truth Enough?* is a book that should be in the hands of every minister and, for that matter, every believer who wants to see truth perpetuated.

On a personal note, it has been my privilege to know Bobby G. Duncan since I was a teenage evangelist coming to his home church to minister. It is with pride that I have watched him develop into an extraordinary preacher, a compassionate pastor, a model denominational leader, and now an author with exceptional writing skills and an uncanny ability to discover and clearly expound the truth. I am honored to call him a very personal friend.

—Homer G. Rhea
Former Editor in Chief
Church of God Publications
Cleveland, Tennessee

❧✦❧

Acknowledgments

Writing a book requires the contribution of many people. Although it is hardly possible to thank everyone by name, there are certain people without whose help this project would have been highly improbable, if not impossible. First, thanks to my wife, Sandra—who will probably never read the finished product, since she has heard me discuss it from every conceivable angle for the past eighteen months or so—for her understanding and support in this undertaking. Thanks also to our two sons, Scott and Shane, the first one a pastor and the second one a member of the church band in his brother's church. They also often listen, albeit sometimes involuntarily, to my frequent reflections, and as much as they joke about that, their observations are usually keen and their input quite thought-provoking.

Sincere appreciation goes to Dr. Mark L. Williams, Church of God general overseer, for taking time in his busy schedule to read this manuscript and to offer his scholarly endorsement. As the newly elected leader of the Church of God in Cleveland, Tennessee, during the 2012 General Assembly in Orlando, Florida, Dr. Williams delivered a powerful message on Josiah and the Book of the Law lost in the Temple. Having just completed the rough draft of this book, I could only sit in amazement as he so astutely and eloquently preached a message on recovering God's Word. It reaffirmed to me that "recovering the truth"—the truth revealed in Jesus Christ—is indeed the message for the church today.

Similarly, thanks to Dr. Tim Hill, general director of World Missions, for giving his valuable time to peruse this work, and for his perceptive and judicious observations. Additionally, thanks to Ron Martin, administrative bishop of the Great Lakes Region; to Dennis Tanner, missionary overseer of Scotland; to Pastors James A. Jones (with whom I've had lengthy discussions on the subject matter contained in this book) and Scott Duncan for their timely and insightful comments.

Many thanks to Homer Rhea Jr.—a seasoned minister, skilled veteran author, and superb church leader—for his willingness to write the Foreword to this book, and for being a sounding board for me for the past year-and-a-half of working on this project. He has been a dear friend for many years and has always been an inspiration to me through his friendship, as well as through his incisive preaching, teaching, and writing.

Also, a deep and heartfelt thanks to Pastor Paul Jones, who for thirty-three years served Parma Park as one of the very best pastors I have ever known. I continue to be blessed by his service as pastor emeritus—now for more than eighteen years—and for his close friendship and dependable support. He has always been the ideal confidant to whom I have continually been able to talk freely. Virtually everything I have written, I have first placed in his hands. A voracious reader and consumer of information, Pastor Jones has always worked at staying on the cutting edge, while at the same time, conscientiously remaining true to God's Word. His spiritual influence on me personally has extended far beyond what words can express.

I am also indebted to longtime parishioner and friend, Stanley Preneta—retired schoolteacher and Korean War veteran—for his skilled analysis of this manuscript and for his attention to detail. He has always challenged my thinking with his probing questions and has always inspired me with his love for truth. He is truly a blessing.

Finally, I am grateful to Lance Colkmire, managing editor of Church of God Publications, and for the entire staff at Pathway Press, for their assistance in seeing to the publication of this book. My prayer is that God's blessings will rest upon them and everyone else who, in some way, contributed to this project. Most of all, may God himself be honored and glorified.

Introduction

One of the most common phrases used today in relationship to ministry and church growth is "think outside the box." If the intended meaning is to think outside of tradition, I understand; if the meaning is to think outside the familiar, I concur; if the meaning is to think outside of what is habitual, I get it. If, on the other hand, in our enthusiasm to become more creative in ministry or to become more appealing to the secular culture, we began to "think outside the Bible," we are destined for failure.

From the time that God spoke to Adam and Eve in Eden concerning the Tree of Life, truth became an elusive quality. For one reason or another, it continues to be—because of Satan's distortions, because people simply do not want anyone telling them how to live their lives, or because so many obsessively seek it in all the wrong places.

For centuries, men searched the celestial heavens to discover truth. They studied cosmic anomalies; they observed the mysteries of the animal kingdom; they scrutinized the complexities of plant life; they carefully analyzed the obscure contemplations of sages and philosophers. Yet, as man plunged the depths of science and philosophy to understand truth, he repeatedly resurfaced empty-handed. Still, regardless of how elusive truth has been, and continues to be, it is only as elusive as a person chooses to make it.

If truth exists, it begs the question asked by Pilate in response to Jesus' statement that He, the Son of God, came into the world to bear witness of the truth (John 18:37-38). Pilate asked, "What is truth?" Although Pilate seemed to pose this question rhetorically, more than likely, he wrestled with it just as others have. *What is truth?* he pondered.

For those who have searched in all the wrong places, the answer to Pilate's question is highly subjective. Conversely, those who have sought for truth in the right place—in God's revealed and written Word—the answer is unmistakable. They have found that truth is God himself, and the words He speaks.

Truth, then, begins and ends with God. Truth is not duplicitous; under no circumstances does it vacillate; it is absolute and unchangeable. Truth has remained the same throughout time and eternity past, being constant in all conditions. It is the same for all people regardless of age, ethnicity, and moral persuasion. But to interpret and apply truth correctly, we must accurately interpret the person and life of Jesus Christ, and apply His principles of conduct to our own lives.

Many years ago, following a message I had delivered on "The Revelation of Jesus Christ" in a church conference, a leading Christian educator came to me, thanked me for selecting that particular subject, and somberly declared, "The message of Jesus is the *lost* message of the church." Since I had been dealing with similar concerns, I interpreted his statement to mean that even though Jesus Christ is preached, Christian ministers and teachers often seem to relegate Him to a lesser role than the one the Bible ascribes to Him. That is, although He may attract some attention, He seems no longer to be at the epicenter of preaching and teaching.

Most troubling is the indication that a growing element within the Christian community in America has systematically reduced Jesus to a side lighted subject overshadowed by a disproportionate emphases on spiritual gifts, signs and wonders, psychology, and in some cases, on marketing expertise and material wealth. The message of Jesus is indeed becoming lost in the very house He built to embrace and disseminate it.

No doubt, we are facing our greatest challenge to interpret truth accurately. Followers of Christ in every period in church history have had their own struggles to maintain biblical balance, but never more than now.

It is not my intention to try to prove the Bible is divinely inspired, inerrant in its formation, and infallible in its message. That is a subject for another time. This brief work assumes the divine authority of the Bible and the commonly accepted tenets of the faith referred to in the Apostles' Creed. Further, I assume that most readers will have a similar persuasion. Consequently, every discussion that follows is set against this backdrop.

In the following chapters, I will explore certain subtle— and sometimes, not so subtle—techniques that Satan uses today to shift attention away from truth within the Christian movement. Although he knows that getting believers to deny Christ is not likely, he is quite aware that coaxing believers into focusing on the human element more than on the person of Christ can be quite effective.

One of the most disturbing passages of Scripture is Revelation 3:20, where Jesus declares, "Behold, I stand at the door and knock. If anyone hears My voice and opens the door, I will come in to him and dine with him, and he with Me." Although this passage has frequently, and quite appropriately, been used as an evangelistic text—Jesus knocking at the door of the human heart, seeking entrance as a personal Savior—close scrutiny indicates that Jesus is speaking primarily to the church at Laodicea.

How is it that the Savior is left standing outside His own professing church seeking admission? As difficult as that scenario is to imagine, there certainly are some easily identifiable reasons for it. For example, Jesus is left outside when the professing church's public image is more important than its spiritual passion, when personal magnetism in the pulpit is esteemed more than the truth, when talent is more desired than spiritual power, and when prosperity and prestige are more recognized than growing in grace. Whatever the reasons, the end result is the same—Jesus excluded from the very house built to honor Him.

Today in America, the larger Christian community is noticeably moving away from the firm foundation of biblical truth, essentially keeping Christ beyond its doors. There is mounting evidence that many church leaders, ministers, and teachers within evangelical circles are thinking more "outside the Bible." Increasingly, church leaders and religious educators seem to view the literal interpretation of the Bible as too restrictive and no longer relevant in our modern culture.

This declining spiritual climate in America's churches is deeply disturbing, and it is the key reason I have made this humble attempt to call readers to a fresh evaluation of truth. My focus in the following pages is not on creativity and innovation in ministry and Christian service, although appropriately utilizing these elements could ably serve the church. Neither is it about thinking "outside the box," even though there is good reason to break away from some of the old worn-out ministry methods that no longer serve us very well. Rather, the principal purpose for this work is about renewing our commitment to staying "inside the box"—that is, the box of truth, the Bible.

There is ample evidence suggesting that the greatest danger facing the church today is not a lack of gifted people, nor even a lack of trained people, but instead, a shortage of people devoted to standing for truth regardless of what it costs them. When the high priest challenged the disciples in Acts 5:28, saying, "Did we not strictly command you not to teach in this name? And look, you have filled Jerusalem with your doctrine," the disciples answered under the threat of continued imprisonment, "We ought to obey God rather than men" (v. 29).

Most, no doubt, would agree that our nation continues to need creativity and innovation in the marketplace. Likewise, many would agree that the Christian church would similarly benefit from the same qualities. However, there lurks the danger in the religious ranks of becoming too dependent on man's resourcefulness to address deeply spiritual issues. The Christian movement in America seems to have come to the place where it delights in man's imagination and cleverness more than in truth. Thinking outside the box often becomes more about what we can do through our own intelligence and cunning as opposed to what God can do through the Holy Spirit's application of truth in our lives.

The crying need for today's generation of believers is to reaffirm faith in Jesus Christ as "the *way*, the *truth*, and the *life*" (John 14:6), and to once again passionately embrace the reality that His kingdom work can only be accomplished through the operation of the Holy Spirit as He brings truth to light, and not by human agency. Man's best efforts done in his own power and by his own initiative fall far short of pleasing God and changing lives. On the other hand, Jesus asserts in 15:7 that if we abide in Him and His words abide is us, nothing shall be impossible. The difference is His established Word—His Word manifested in Jesus Christ, who *is* Truth.

The following manuscript rests largely upon Jesus' words in John 8:32, "You shall know the truth, and the truth shall make you free," and Paul's appeal in Philippians 3:10, "That I may know Him and the power of His resurrection."

Knowing the truth and *knowing* Him, experientially, are synonymous. Spiritual freedom only comes through this knowledge and experience. This truth in Jesus Christ—foreshadowed in the Old Testament and revealed in the New Testament—is God's gift to fallen man. We cannot add anything to it that would enhance it; neither can we take anything away from it that would ultimately diminish it.

Our present peace and our eternal future both depend on a correct interpretation and application of truth. If anyone seeking truth overlooks Jesus, or distorts the vision of His person, the consequences will be disastrous. If, on the other hand, sincere seekers properly interpret and apply truth as Christ revealed it, God promises joy instead of sorrow, life instead of death, and reward instead of punishment.

1

❧❧

The Word of Truth

"So He humbled you, allowed you to hunger, and fed you with manna which you did not know nor did your fathers know, that He might make you know that man shall not live by bread alone; but man lives by every word that proceeds from the mouth of the Lord" (Deut. 8:3).

Growing up in the rural South provided my four brothers and me memories for a lifetime. As I often reflect on those formative years, I am reminded of how blessed we were—not just because of the outdoors, the hunting and fishing, and the span of pastures and woods in which to play, but also because of the dynamics of our family life. Most important of all, God blessed us with two loving, godly parents.

Dad and Mom both grew up on small farms and married in the middle of the Depression. Like so many from that generation, they had a great appreciation for the simple things in life. They also had a deep love for God and a passion for His Word.

Just after the beginning of World War II, Dad and Mom moved to Mobile, Alabama, where Dad had secured a job as a welder for Gulf Shipbuilding in Chickasaw. After settling into one of the company homes there, he and Mom, along with my two oldest brothers, began attending the nearby Krafton Church of God. There they sat under two remarkable pastors—Pastors Wilson and Spencer. Both had reputations as excellent pulpiteers.

Pastor Wilson, a former lawyer, was an outstanding Bible teacher who placed great emphasis on Bible study for his parishioners. Perhaps there was no other pastor, before or after, who influenced Dad and Mom to study the Bible more than this man did. Based on their own stories of this period in their lives, this was the time and place when both experienced rapid spiritual growth and became deeply rooted in God's Word. Their love and passion for truth became the all-encompassing element of life and permanently influenced five sons.

Some of the most memorable times for me growing up in the '50s and '60s were those evenings sitting together with my parents and brothers in a small living room participating in family devotions. Our parents determined that the instructions their spiritual leaders had given to them, they would conscientiously pass along to their children, believing the Bible to be the very foundation of life. They looked for ways to make God's Word easy to study and understand, and determined to keep the entire family engaged in interesting discussions about it.

I fondly recall how Dad and Mom employed two particular methods to keep our attention focused on the reading of the Bible during family devotions. First, they wisely involved everyone who could read, giving every school-age child his turn at sharing the Word. Second, they made it a guessing game. Whichever family member may have been reading the Scriptures on any given evening, that person would not give the name of the book, the chapter from which it came, and the number of verses read. The reader would leave that for the others to guess.

When we were small children, the exercise was truly a *guessing* game. And we kept guessing until we had nailed down the missing information. As the years passed and we all learned more about the Bible, we moved away from simply guessing and often began identifying portions of Scripture that had now become so much part of our lives.

The effect of those early years of Bible studies—studies that began in our home and continued in the Sunday school classrooms and in the sanctuary of a small evangelical church—so influenced five siblings that all continue to serve the Lord today, along with children and grandchildren. Although Dad and Mom had little formal education, they experienced the life-changing power of God's Word and did not rest until they had taught the truth, not only to their children, but also to many others privileged to hear them minister as Sunday school teachers.

Sadly, church leaders and parents today teach less and less of the Bible, believing that we can no longer embrace it as authoritative and absolute. Even though many question its relevancy to our modern culture, the Bible remains the only true guide by which we are able to safely navigate the often-dangerous waters of life.

Not only is the Bible the guide for our journey of faith, it is also the guide in our quest for personal holiness, for righteousness. Jesus said, "You are already clean because of the word which I have spoken to you" (John 15:3). He prayed for His disciples, "Sanctify them by Your truth. Your word is truth" (17:17).

At the very heart of man's existence is a common necessity to conform, in some manner, to a set standard. In addition to his inherent need to live by a particular standard, there rests deep inside his innermost being a conscience—a conscience that assists in determining the acceptable standard by which he lives his life.

Although God surely works through man's conscience, the conscience is not completely trustworthy, since it is not always quick to recognize the difference between good and evil. It is not always as decisive as it needs to be, and is not always dependable in making necessary judgments. The reason, of course, is that the conscience is susceptible to becoming contaminated and, according to Paul, can even become seared (1 Tim. 4:2).

This brings us back to the necessity of God's written Word. Man simply cannot make critical judgments about life and death on his own merit. Knowledge is much too limited, and the conscience is not always a perfect guide. "For the commandment is a lamp; and the law a light; reproofs of instruction are the way of life" (Prov. 6:23).

God has always set forth—by word, by act, or by example—truth as the standard by which He expects man to live his life. He has never left Himself without a witness. Although human nature has always nudged man in the direction of determining his own concept of truth—which is usually not truth at all—God has made truth clear in every age to all who would genuinely seek for it. He has always given instructions for trusting and serving in ways to which people at every stage in history could relate. Never has He left man to speculate abstractly on the right standard. If man chooses to participate in such speculations, he does so of his own volition, at his own risk, and to his own injury.

In early history, God revealed His standard of truth through personal characters such as Enoch, Noah, and Abraham. Following these personal testimonies, came the spoken and written words, typically expressed through ceremonial observances because of the shortage of written words. As God's plan of eternal salvation continued to develop, He used prophets and teachers. Finally, the eternal God fully and perfectly manifested the standard of truth in the person of His Son Jesus Christ. "And without controversy great is the mystery of godliness: God was manifested in the flesh, justified in the Spirit, seen by angels, preached among the Gentiles, believed on in the world, received up in glory" (1 Tim. 3:16).

Because of the unsettling and convicting nature of truth, our postmodern culture has taken a calculated jab at it in an effort to relegate it to the dustbin of history as an outdated worldview whose useful life has ended. The intellectual elite, the mainstream media, and even acclaimed theologians frequently declare that the truth revealed in Jesus Christ is obsolete and, therefore, no longer applicable to people within a highly developed society. To them, anyone's concept of truth is strictly a matter of personal choice and, therefore, should not influence the attitudes and standards of others.

Still, there *is* truth. Some may dismiss it, others may fiercely attack it, and many may carelessly compromise it. They may question it, criticize it, deride and disclaim it, but no one can destroy it. Truth can only become a casualty to people who reject it. It always survives critics and dissenters because God, who *is* Truth, endures. Truth can no more be dismantled than God can be removed from His holy throne.

Truth, however, is not an abstract concept. To declare that truth exists and that it is timeless is one thing; to make it personal and relevant is something entirely different. Although many accept that God is truth, the word He speaks is truth, and the work He does is truth, the question remains, "How does that relate to us?"

To make truth applicable to His disenfranchised creation, God sent His Son Jesus Christ in the flesh to the earth. "And the Word became flesh and dwelt among us, and we beheld His glory, the glory as of the only begotten of the Father, full of grace and truth" (John 1:14). Jesus became the embodiment and revelation of truth.

Consequently, it is impossible for man to simultaneously accept truth and reject Christ. The two cannot be mutually exclusive. If God is truth, and if the fullness of the Godhead dwells bodily in Jesus Christ, then it makes sense that to reject Christ is to reject truth.

The powers of darkness have always attacked God's Word—its inspiration, inerrancy, and infallibility—in every way imaginable, and from every quarter. Throughout history, Satan has launched aggressive frontal assaults on the Word, attacking it in such ways that in some countries owning a Bible has been, and continues to be, a capital offense. Even during times when the forces of evil have tried to eradicate the printed Word, it has not only survived, but has engendered an even greater hunger for it.

For example, the prohibition on the Bible behind the Iron Curtain in past decades only seemed to strengthen the resolve of believers. When the Berlin Wall came down and the Iron Curtain rose, we discovered that untold numbers of believers populated these communist countries, believers who had only grown more determined to serve God through years of religious persecution.

As effective as Satan's assaults have often been in keeping many from having access to the Bible, his most effective attacks against truth usually come in more subtle ways. That is, even though he will continue to try to destroy the Bible through physical force as long as he has a position of power, he usually attempts to extinguish the fire of truth through human reasoning, philosophical questions, and scientific speculations. This approach is perhaps his most effective scheme.

Man's futile attempts to discover truth through human means remind us that genuine power—eternal power—is not inherent in man. Rather, it resides in God, and in God alone. So powerful, in fact, is the Word, that Jesus said when heaven and earth would pass away in their present forms, His Word would remain. It will remain whether people accept or reject it.

As important as trusting God is, the function and fulfillment of truth does not depend on the *faith* of man; it depends on the *faithfulness* of God. "If we are faithless, He remains faithful; He cannot deny Himself" (2 Tim. 2:13). Although unbelieving people keep God from working in their behalf, not all the unbelief in the world can keep God from fulfilling His Word. He cannot lie (Heb. 6:18).

God has firmly established truth in the earth, and has revealed it as the only solid footing we have in a world of shifting, unstable ground. Whether people choose to trust Him or not to trust Him, and whether they choose to obey Him or not to obey Him, He will not change. Because God is immutable, truth is immutable. Man's faith is shakable because of the human element; God's faithfulness is unshakable because of His perfection.

In John 6:47-58, Jesus taught that He was the Bread of Life, and that if anyone wanted eternal life, that person had to "eat His flesh and drink His blood" (see vv. 53-54). This was a strange saying, and something the Jews had never heard before. They murmured at the very idea that Jesus called Himself "the bread which came down from heaven" (v. 58), and struggled even more at they thought that they would have to eat His flesh and drink His blood.

Jesus knew His words were hard for His disciples to receive and asked them, "Does this offend you?" (v. 61). For many, it did offend them, for John noted, "From that time many of His disciples went back and walked with Him no more" (v. 66).

In response to the departure of many who had previously followed Him, Jesus turned to the Twelve and asked, "Do you also want to go away?" Then Simon Peter, with all his emotional volatility and glaring human weaknesses, answered, "Lord, to whom shall we go? You have the words of eternal life" (v. 68).

After defending His eternal association with His Father in John 5:19-47 before the Jews, Jesus challenged His listeners in verse 39, "You search the Scriptures, for in them you think you have eternal life; and these are they which testify of Me."

With all the world's libraries filled with great works of literature, history, and philosophy, not a single volume, nor even a combination of volumes, answers man's deepest questions and needs. Only the Bible does that. There has never been a book written, other than the Bible, that reveals the existence of a ubiquitous, all-knowing, all-powerful, and immutable God who "so loved the world that He gave His only begotten Son . . . " for the salvation of all who would believe on Him (3:16). Neither can there be found a solitary volume of secular history that promised us a Messiah capable of securing our perfect righteousness. In essence, the only way we can know about life, death, the return of Christ, and the resurrection—about eternal hope in a hopeless world—is through discovering it in the Bible.

God has established His Word for all eternity. "Forever, O Lord, Your word is settled in heaven" (Ps. 119:89). The divine inspiration of the Bible, its inerrancy, and its infallibility assures us that through living in Jesus Christ, days will be brighter, life will be more fulfilling, problems will be less threatening, joy will abound, and the future will be more rewarding than the past. The solid rock of truth will never tremble under those who embrace it and put their trust in Him who *is* Truth.

2

⤳⤫

Truth Lost

*"My people are destroyed for lack of knowledge.
Because you have rejected knowledge, I also will reject
you from being priest for Me; because you have forgotten
the law of your God, I also will forget your children"*
(Hos. 4:6).

The time—circa 640 B.C.; the place—Jerusalem; the
event—repairing of Solomon's Temple; the king—Josiah.

According to 2 Kings 22 and 2 Chronicles 34, Josiah began to reign in Jerusalem when he was only eight years old
and reigned for thirty-one years. Both accounts state, "And
he did what was right in the sight of the Lord, and walked in
all the ways of his father David; he did not turn aside to the
right hand or to the left" (v. 2).

The history of the Israelites is mingled with references to
kings not doing right in the sight of the Lord and not walk-
ing in the ways of David. While the kings of Israel tended to
follow this evil course, more of the kings of Judah inclined
their hearts toward God. Interestingly, in at least one case,
Amaziah's reign, the record states, "And he did what was
right in the sight of the Lord, but not with a loyal heart"
(2 Chron. 25:2).

Although Amaziah's story is one of good intentions, unfortunately it is also one of halfhearted actions—a reign of mediocrity. Josiah's narrative, however, is much different from that of evil rulers, and appreciably different from that of mediocre leaders. He proved himself a guardian of truth, conscientious, determined, and persevering, "not turn[ing] aside to the right hand or to the left" (34:2).

It is not unusual that, if greatness is thrust upon someone so young, an inflated appraisal of self often follows. This was not the case with this young king. Rather, while Josiah was still young, he began to conscientiously seek after God. The spiritual environment surrounding him, his response to God's call, and God's enablement were destined to make him one of Judah's greatest kings. Although his challenges appeared overwhelming, he did not stumble in his commitment to righteous principles.

For over 330 years, Judah existed as an independent kingdom. A little more than one hundred years earlier, the Assyrians had taken Israel captive, ostensibly ending her existence as a nation, and now, Judah's days were fast approaching. In spite of God's repeated warnings through the prophets, His fatherly chastisements, and His merciful interventions, the people grew worse and worse, giving themselves wholly to idolatry. Into this dark era of spiritual and moral decay stepped the child king, Josiah.[1]

Interestingly, the influences in his early life seem to have been unfavorable—certainly the example of his father, Amon.

Therefore, it is reasonable to conclude that Josiah, even at his early age, had some inkling of his father's wickedness. Furthermore, he must have heard the stories of his grandfather, King Manasseh, and his utter depravity. Perhaps Josiah's mother, Jedidah, was an exception. Surely, someone had a positive influence on him, and who would be more likely to have that effect than his own mother?

Regardless of the evil influence of his father, the wicked history of his grandfather, and the sheer idolatry of the entire nation, Josiah determined not to bow down to idols but to follow God with his whole heart.

Second Chronicles 34:3 informs us that Josiah, in his eighth year, began to seek after the God of David his father. That is, as early as the age of sixteen, he began to show signs of deep devotion to the God of Jacob and a single-hearted commitment to righteousness.

The same verse tells us that in his twelfth year—at age twenty—he began pursuing a course of action to purge Judah and Jerusalem from the high places, its groves, and its carved and molten images. No doubt, he had to proceed cautiously, considering that idolatry had long since become entrenched in Judah's culture. Immoral pagan practices—such as Baal worship, human sacrifices, and sodomite houses—abounded. Surely, a strong and influential religious-political party powerfully ruled to ensure that this corrupt system survived. Josiah certainly must have found himself up against what now had become an established institution.

Perhaps with little support, Josiah moved ahead with his acts of reformation. His convictions ran deep, and he no doubt cringed at the thought of allowing the grossly sinful practices common in Judah to continue any longer. He had now reached an age where he could reasonably make judgments on his own that affected the entire nation. This he did, continuing these reforms into his eighteenth year of being king.

Until this time—at twenty-six years of age—Josiah had forged ahead without a copy of the Book of the Law to consult. However, without the written Law, he knew enough through certain influences, and had been so touched by God, that his conscience was in good working order. Still, without a copy of the Law, his reforms were more forced than voluntary. More than likely, he had many constituents who followed along, but did so reluctantly. No doubt, his reforms did not come without significant sacrifice on his part and on the part of those in agreement with him.

What is so deeply disturbing about the first part of this narrative is the absence of God's written Word. The Book of the Law that existed at that time was probably the first five books of Moses (the Pentateuch), or at least the largest portion of them. Since copying such a volume would have been a monumental undertaking for anyone, very few existed, other than perhaps the Temple copy. Still, the solemn responsibility to maintain a copy of the Law rested in the hands of Israel's leaders. God entrusted them to see that His Word remained alive.

As to when the Book of the Law had been misplaced, we can only guess. More than likely, it happened during the lengthy reign of Josiah's grandfather, Manasseh, over fifty years earlier. It is not likely to have happened before that time, considering that Manasseh's father was the godly king Hezekiah.

According to Deuteronomy 31, just before the death of Moses, he transcribed the Law that God had given to him. After writing it down, he delivered it into the hands of the priests and commanded them on this order:

> At the end of every seven years, at the appointed time in the year of release, at the Feast of Tabernacles, when all Israel comes to appear before the Lord your God in the place which He chooses, you shall read this law before all Israel in their hearing. Gather the people together, men and women and little ones, and the stranger who is within your gates, that they may hear and that they may learn to fear the Lord your God and carefully observe all the words of this law, and that their children, who have not known it, may hear and learn to fear the Lord your God (vv. 10-13).

Furthermore, in verses 25 and 26, Moses instructed the Levites—the bearers of the ark of the covenant—to take the Book of the Law and place it inside the ark that it would remain there for a witness against them in any wrongdoing.

Earlier, in chapter 17, Moses announced that when the children of Israel came into the Land of Promise, God would set a king over them. In addition to the responsibility of the anticipated king to protect himself from polygamy and greed,

Moses declared that "he shall write for himself a copy of this law in a book, from the one before the priests, the Levites" (v. 18).

Although surely some kings did that, most did not. Wicked kings would have had no interest in maintaining a copy of the Law since they had no desire to live by it.[2] Even certain good kings, with all good intentions, probably never got around to making their own copy. Over time, interest faded and negligence ensued. The priests functioned according to long-standing traditions, and slowly, almost imperceptibly, knowledge of the letter of the Law and a sincere concept of the spirit of the Law disappeared.

Today, it would seem inconceivable that within a local church body there would be no Bible found. The idea that a pastor and congregation would even attempt to negotiate the often rough and rocky paths of the Christian walk without the Bible as a guide would be unthinkable. Is it plausible that a God-called pastor would take the reins of spiritual and ecclesiastical oversight, operating only with a fleeting concept of biblical doctrine? We would like to think not.

Although there are some religious leaders who do just that, it is not possible for anyone, however capable and charismatic, to passionately and properly lead the body of Christ with only a fading memory of truth. There are too many complexities in life, too many challenges, and too many divine instructions to get by with just a passing reference to the Bible.

Yet today, this is precisely what we see happening in the religious world around us. The infallibility of the Bible is rejected, the sinless nature of Christ is questioned, the reality of the Holy Spirit is doubted, and the truth of the Resurrection is denied. Many pastors and church members continue to operate churches based on hollow religious tradition, personal ideology, and grossly distorted concepts of right and wrong. The truth revealed in God's Word has become highly subjective—that is, open to personal and private interpretation with no accountability.

As improbable as it seems today, God's Word has become "lost" in the very house built in its honor. Who would have thought that the Book of the Law in Josiah's time would become lost in the Temple? Yet, it had. And even as we wonder how that could have happened then, we must admit that losing God's Word today in His church is even harder to imagine—harder to conceive because, in Josiah's time, few copies existed, perhaps only one. In our time, Bibles are plentiful—in a vast array of colors, in many translations, and in convenient sizes for all. More than likely, practically every person in America has access to a Bible, although few people seem interested in reading it. As abundant as the written Word is, it remains lost to hearts and minds because of disinterest.

If the only thing substantial in this world is truth, if the only unshakable foundation is truth, and if the only way to life itself is truth, then we can ill-afford to lay it aside, arbitrarily dismissing it from our lives. The Word of God lost in God's house is a contradiction with unimaginable consequences. Losing the Word of Truth in the very environment established to guard and propagate it ultimately means the continuance of sin with no promise of forgiveness, conflicts with no serious and lasting means of resolution, confusion with no hope of clarity, and defeat with no assurance of recovery.

The very thought that Judah had gotten down to only a single copy of the Law, and that copy misplaced, is disturbing, to say the least. It is reasonable to think that scribes would have busied themselves making copies of the Law under the direction of kings and priests. Priorities had apparently changed, and the most important work—producing and proclaiming God's covenant to the people—became unimportant.

Josiah conscientiously began reforming Judah early in his reign as king, but until the recovery of the Book of the Law, those reforms only scratched the surface. The king methodically went about his business of removing the visible objects associated with idolatry, but the nature of the nation remained unchanged. What Judah needed was something much deeper than just the memory of religious ceremony, of external observance. Judah needed the whole truth of God's covenant so that His words would reach deep inside the hearts of the people, reveal all that was wrong, and change their corrupt nature. Anything short of the restoration of God's Word would have kept Him at arm's length and, consequently, would have left the people of Judah to their own devices, to provide for their own necessities, to fight their own battles, and to find their own way.

Like this notable time in Judah's history, truth today has been laid aside in a backroom of God's house, collecting dust and hidden by volumes of proposals designed by man. Although truth ultimately will triumph, for now, man adjusts it to accommodate his nearsighted objectives. Consequently, God's Word must be recovered. If it continues to lie hidden away from sight and mind, the religious landscape in America will look more and more like a barren wasteland, unable to sustain a population hungry for spiritual nourishment.

If the larger Christian body in America is to experience spiritual restoration, it first has to return to truth, to the indestructible Word of God. Jesus Christ—His person and work—has to once again become the focal point of preaching and teaching, and not just another component in a religious system much too encumbered by the human element. Yet, at best, there are distractions, and at worst, disillusionment and deception that keep that from happening. Let us consider some of these troubling concerns in the following chapters.

3

⪻⪼

Truth Trumped by Tradition

This testimony is true. Therefore rebuke them sharply,
that they may be sound in the faith, not giving heed to
Jewish fables and commandments of men who turn from
the truth (Titus 1:13-14).

Traditions—usually unwritten beliefs or customs handed down from one generation to another—are common to all people and daily play a significant role in social and religious life. Such a shared system of ideas is one of the major components in keeping families connected through the years, and one of the very things that keeps religious communities united over time and through adversity.

In the filial sense, traditions have to do with attitudes, ideas, principles, and backgrounds that promote a sense of identity, intimacy, and security within a particular family structure. In the religious sense, traditions have to do with the same things but also involve styles of worship and prayer, and methods employed to accomplish Christian service. Whatever the traditions, they refresh our memory, gather us in a common setting, and help establish community.

Many years ago during a visit to see my parents in south Mississippi, I took a little extra time and drove the additional twenty miles back to my mother's old home place, once a small farm producing mostly cotton and corn. The old familiar weather-beaten, mostly unpainted house (the front door and window frames had been painted some years earlier) had stood for more than a hundred years and held countless memories for me and for many kinfolk as well.

The large frame and time-honored farm dwelling was located in an area of rolling green hills interspersed with pine thickets and giant oak trees, all unevenly divided by a number of small streams and creeks. In earlier years, the well-spaced and neatly kept neighboring farms offered a genuine sense of community and served to compliment the appearance and intrigue of the family farm.

I remember roaming the familiar hills and hollows there as a boy and hunting in the wooded areas with my father, brothers, uncles, and cousins. This was the place where my immediate family often spent Thanksgivings and Christmases with an incredible number of extended family members, many of whom we only had the opportunity to see on those special occasions.

My memories of those holiday gatherings and meals still kindle my senses of smell and taste—the smell of wood burning in the fireplace, the aroma of spices used in cooking, and the delightful taste of the food itself.

During those special times of getting together, the old farm displayed a personality all its own. The old frame house with its informal atmosphere rang with conversation and laughter, while the spacious yard and old barn played host to rowdy groups of excited children. We made memories without a passing thought as to how these memories would affect us throughout our lives.

On this particular day as I walked up into the spacious yard shaded by its many pecan trees, a real pang of sadness smote my heart. The old weather-beaten house which had stood the test of time for so long and had braved so many storms, had finally relinquished its hold on existence. I noticed that the back part of the house had completely collapsed, and the old stained tin roof had at last yielded to the persistent winds that, for so long, had ripped at its edges. Grass had grown up around the hedges that once had been kept neatly trimmed.

In those moments that I stood looking and thinking, I understood I was seeing an old landmark of family history slowly fade into extinction. I heard no laughter floating across the expansive yard and saw no smoke rising from the crumbling chimney. The only sounds were those of a few cows on a distant hillside and the rustling of the leaves in the trees as the wind softly whispered its refrain.

For a few fleeting seconds, I tried to re-create those happy days of yesteryear in my mind. As if a large movie screen appeared before my eyes, I imagined I could see the men sitting by the fireplace, the women folk rushing around the kitchen, and the children scrambling over bales of hay and scampering around the yard and through the woods.

Suddenly the reality of the present jolted me from my brief excursion to the past. The house *had* fallen into decay.

The people *were* gone. The weeds *had* taken over. All the unforgettable activities of this old farm were nothing more now than memories—intangible and haunting, yet so real and fraught with meaning.

Still to this day, when the remaining kinfolk get together for a reunion, the conversations naturally drift back to a time and place that held us firmly together. For us, the traditions of a time long ago are still treasured—valuable beyond measure.

Just as I frequently take sentimental journeys along the path of family history, I similarly recall a little frame church building in McComb, Mississippi, a small town of about twelve thousand people during my early years. Dad and Mom had moved there following World War II so Dad could take a job with the Illinois Central Railroad, McComb's largest employer. They were among a handful of believers who helped organize a church there in 1951, and spent the rest of their lives serving God in that venue. It was there that I sat under many influential pastors and remarkable Sunday school teachers determined to teach children and searching teens the truth of God's unadulterated Word.

Fortunately, I had grown up with both rich family traditions and with valuable religious traditions. I still largely hold those traditions as cherished possessions. Expressing the value of traditions, the apostle Paul said, "Therefore, brethren, stand fast and hold the traditions which you were taught, whether by word or our epistle" (2 Thess. 2:15).

As important as traditions are—filial, religious, or otherwise—and as much as they affect our lives, we must understand they are not only *apt* to change, they *will* change. Old traditions are replaced or modified ever so slowly by succeeding generations whose priorities and lifestyles significantly differ from those of their parents and grandparents. At least some of what may be traditional for my generation will probably not be traditional for my grandchildren's generation and the generations that follow.

Regardless of how much people cling to the traditions that resonate with them, and regardless of how enduring those traditions are, they are still in flux. People adjust them to the changing times, adapting them for the sake of convenience, or out of necessity. Likewise, truth is enduring, but conversely, it is not subject to adjustments and adaptations. It is not open to modification and is not influenced by priorities and lifestyles.

Disturbingly, today's generation has little understanding of historical Christianity, of biblical truth. Many people have never opened a Bible or entered a place of worship. Consequently, the challenge for professing believers steeped in church traditions to minister to others has become a daunting task. Traditions that may have served us well in the past—prayer style, worship style, preaching style, ministry methodology, and denominational dogmas—are less and less effective. Although that may not always be the case, it has certainly become so in America's rapidly shifting culture. As important as our preferences may be to us, we must realize that worship customs and ministry techniques are not in themselves sufficient for the task of reaching and discipling the harvest of souls before us.

Thirteen times in the New Testament, some form of the word *tradition* is used, and in only three instances is the word used in a positive sense. The problem, however, is not so much our traditions as it is equating them with biblical truth. They may assist us in our worship and fellowship, and they may provide familiar means to participate in Christian service, but under no circumstances are we to elevate our religious customs to the level of truth. Truth—the message of creation and redemption, accomplished and applied in Jesus Christ, His cross and resurrection—is indeed the only constant in this equation.

The Pharisees are good examples of professing believers and worshipers given more to the external features of worship and service than to the inward embracing of these elements. Christ said to them:

> "Well did Isaiah prophesy of you hypocrites, as it is written: 'This people honors Me with their lips, but their heart is far from Me. And in vain they worship Me, teaching as doctrines the commandments of men.' For laying aside the commandment of God, you hold the tradition of men—the washing of pitchers and cups, and many other such things you do. . . . All too well you reject the commandment of God, that you may keep your tradition" (Mark 7:6-9).

Christ did not criticize them for having traditions, because He knew they were a valuable part of life, and not a problem in themselves. However, He did censure them for ignoring God's commandments in order to keep their traditions. Again, the problem was not so much their religious customs as it was the placing of the customs of men above the laws of God. He cried against them saying, "You reject the commandment of God, that you may keep your tradition" (v. 9). In verse 13, He declared, "Making the word of God of no effect through your tradition which you have handed down."

Religion has always been popular. Since the beginning of time, there has been that mysterious something in man's heart that inclines toward the supernatural. Although man frequently thwarts God's purpose for his life, there remains the desire for something intangible and unexplainable— hence, the appeal of religion. However, religion alone is only a belief system having more to do with ceremony than with relationship. Religion is an organizational structure, a set of rules, an accepted creed that, although perhaps temporarily appeasing an aching conscience, does little for man's innermost being.

The Old Testament Law given to Moses served Israel well for the time frame in which God placed it. However necessary the Law was in God establishing a covenant relationship with His people, it had no inherent power to change lives. Yet, it fit perfectly in God's plan by preparing for the coming Messiah, being "a shadow of the good things to come" (Heb. 10:1). In relationship to the old and new covenants, the writer to the Hebrews said:

It was symbolic for the present time in which both gifts and sacrifices are offered which cannot make him who performed the service perfect in regard to the conscience—concerned only with foods and drinks, various washings, and fleshly ordinances imposed until the time of reformation. But Christ came as High Priest of the good things to come, with the greater and more perfect tabernacle not made with hands, that is, not of this creation. Not with the blood of goats and calves, but with His own blood He entered the Most Holy Place once for all, having obtained eternal redemption (9:9-12).

God never intended the Old Testament system to remain in effect. The truth revealed in the sacrifices and ceremonies never changed, but the system itself was the medium God used to bring the truth to light—the medium that served its purpose until Jesus Christ came as the perfect sacrifice and the perfect High Priest. The system itself changed dramatically, so much, in fact, that it completely unsettled the Jewish hierarchy. Still, the change did not alter the truth; it only revealed it more fully.

In His Sermon on the Mount, Jesus said, "Do not think that I came to destroy the Law or the Prophets. I did not come to destroy but to fulfill" (Matt. 5:17). By now, though, the Jews had come to honor and worship the system more than the God of truth, and yet, the system was but a form of godliness. The Old Testament system had become a sacred institution worthy to be maintained at all costs, even at the expense of truth.

Churches, temples, and worship centers dot the landscape throughout the world. Many people claim and profess godliness, but often their worship is only a formality, an outward profession, and a superficial appearance of godliness. In reality, they do not sincerely trust and serve God. Perhaps they go through the motions of praying, believing, worshiping, and serving, but expressions are perfunctory and hollow. They refuse to allow Christ inside their hearts and lives. In theory, they are Christians, but in practice, they deny the power of God, the power of the Cross, the power of the Resurrection, and the power of the Holy Spirit.

Regrettably, man usually finds just enough benefits in religion to curb his appetite for a deep and lasting personal relationship with Jesus Christ, but not enough to profoundly change his life. And this misdirection leads us to one of the major difficulties with religious tradition. That is, religion alone is often more damaging than no religion at all because, ultimately, it distracts from the person of Jesus Christ by offering a soothing alternative. The alternative may presumably embrace Christ, but it does so only in an abstract sense. The focus of worship and service comes largely to bear upon religious ritual itself; it does not lend itself to inward change and practical godliness. The danger, then, rests in embracing a powerless belief system that brings with it a false sense of security.

This was Christ's precise concern when He challenged the Pharisees. They knew Jewish religious law in minute detail. Intellectually, they excelled, strictly adhering to the traditions of their fathers. Spiritually, they failed. They repeatedly focused on the letter of the Law at the expense of the spirit of the Law.

First Samuel 4:3 provides a good example of what happens when God's people embrace tradition more than truth: "And when the people had come into the camp, the elders of Israel said, 'Why has the Lord defeated us today before the Philistines? Let us bring the ark of the covenant of the Lord from Shiloh to us, that when it comes among us it may save us from the hand of our enemies.'"

The high priest, Eli, had grown old. Carelessly, he had failed to restrain his sons, Hophni and Phinehas, only lightly reprimanding them for their abject wickedness. Serving as priests with their father, they had plundered the sacrifices offered to God, demanding the best parts of the offerings for themselves. In addition, they openly defiled the women selected for tabernacle service, bringing an even greater reproach upon the priesthood. The light of God's presence had now become but a fading and flickering glow, hardly noticeable at all.

In this deteriorating spiritual climate, and in view of Israel's glaring signs of weakness, the Philistines arrayed themselves in battle against them. This barbaric people had been a constant threat to the national security of Israel, and now, the time had come for their complete triumph.

As the battle raged, the tide of victory began to turn against Israel. After about four thousand men fell before the enemy, Israel's defeat seemed inevitable. Not willing yet to give up the fight, the elders came up with what they believed to be the perfect solution: "Get the ark of the covenant!"

The ark of the covenant was a symbol, or material sign, of spiritual truth. It represented the presence, majesty, holiness, and protection of the invisible King of Israel. The leaders of Israel approached God by way of the ark. The ark led the way into battle. The priest carrying the ark stood in the midst of Jordan while God's people crossed into the land of Canaan. In essence, the ark of the covenant was the visible representation of the invisible God.

After having tasted sweet victory repeatedly in the shadow of the ark, the elders of Israel now succumbed to the temptation to trust in the symbol itself. Notice their words, "When *it* comes among us *it* may save us from the hand of our enemies" (v. 3). After all that God had done for His children, He now finds them trusting in His symbol instead of in Him.

Clearly, there exists a conflict between the shadow and the substance. Israel placed her faith in the mystical ark and foolishly believed that the symbol could save them. They were not looking to God. They only looked to themselves and to the work of their own hands.

This is a graphic example of how God's people misuse their faith. Tradition gains honor while truth takes a backseat. When the symbol receives an undue share of attention in comparison with the truth, the symbol becomes an idol. It is mockery when a material emblem that represents God can actually become the focus of attention and worship, ultimately defeating its true purpose.

Again, this is but a form of godliness that distracts from the true and living God. Symbols are useful only if we rightfully use them and hold them subordinate to spiritual truth. We must never view them as sacred.

Surely, people of faith find some measure of comfort in rituals and religious ceremonies, but ultimately, those formalities are only superficial signs and observances that cannot wash away sins and cannot purge the conscience from dead works. Standing alone, they do not promote spiritual worship, and they do not lead to sincere, sacrificial service in God's kingdom.

Regardless of how much value we place in a particular ecclesiastical system, such a system cannot save us any more than the ark of the covenant could save Israel. Amazingly, when the ark arrived in the midst of the battle, Israel suffered defeat and the Philistines took the ark. Shortly afterward, Eli, having heard that the glory had departed from Israel, fell from the place where he sat, broke his neck, and died.

The answer was not in the "ark of the Lord," because it had no inherent power. The answer was in the "Lord of the ark."[1] The ark only represented the God of Israel. We cannot expect to find the miraculous power of God encapsulated in a physical object or in the traditions of man. Such glorious power resides only in God himself.

Paul knew from his conversion experience on the road to Damascus that he could never become fulfilled and perfect through a religious sacrament. He knew that his only hope of eternal life rested in a personal relationship with Jesus Christ. He declared:

> Yet indeed I also count all things loss for the excellence of the knowledge of Christ Jesus my Lord, for whom I have suffered the loss of all things, and count them as rubbish, that I may gain Christ and be found in Him, not having my own righteousness, which is from the law, but that which is through faith in Christ, the righteousness which is from God by faith; that I may know Him and the power of His resurrection, and the fellowship of His sufferings, being conformed to His death, if, by any means, I may attain to the resurrection from the dead (Phil. 3:8-11).

When he used the words in verse 10, "That I may know Him," he spoke of a personal and intimate knowledge that he knew he could never gain through religious observance, but only through direct personal communion with the Lord. His cry was that he would constantly increase in the personal knowledge of his Savior, expressing that this knowledge rested, not on religious traditions, but on the truth revealed in Jesus Christ alone.

If the church is to experience spiritual renewal, it has to get beyond a form of godliness—beyond superficial ceremonies, token religious performances, symbolic rituals—and earnestly search His Word and His face. It is not about a customary worship practice, it is about His divine personage and power. Too often, we find ourselves worshiping our worship style instead of God—having faith in our ability to believe as opposed to simply believing, and rejoicing over our up-to-date and better-than-the-other-church's evangelistic methods, instead of rejoicing that our names are written in heaven.

Just as family traditions generally contribute to family health and stability, religious traditions do the same. However, these traditions alone have never been able to ensure family or spiritual health and stability for anyone. Religious ceremonies may bring a shallow peace, and they may even provoke legitimate thoughts of God, but they can never "cleanse [man's] conscience from dead works" (Heb. 9:14), and they can never ignite a burning hope in the power of God's forgiveness and in the power of Christ's resurrection.

According to Paul, the antithesis to religious tradition is *relationship*—a personal relationship with Jesus Christ, the Creator of all things and the giver of life. A person cannot build a fulfilling spiritual life on religion, but he can build such a life through cultivating an intimate relationship with his Savior.

Whereas religion depends on church fathers, relationship depends on God our Father. While religion embraces the cross of Christ, relationship embraces the Christ of the cross. Religion announces a ceremony; relationship announces a personal Savior. Where religion looks to an ecclesiastical system as the final authority, relationship looks to Christ as the head of the Church, preeminent in all things.

As long as we hold religious traditions subordinate to biblical truth, those traditions are able to serve us in some measure. However, once we give more attention to our preferred styles of prayer and worship, and to our dogmas and ministry methods than we do to God's Word and to true spirituality, we have dealt truth an undeserving blow, and have cheated ourselves in the process.

4

✥

Truth Distorted by Human Philosophy

Beware lest anyone cheat you through philosophy and empty deceit, according to the tradition of men, according to the basic principles of the world, and not according to Christ (Col. 2:8).

Bertrand Russell, one of the most celebrated philosophers of the twentieth century, saw philosophy as a discipline suspended somewhere between science and theology. He taught that all definite knowledge belonged to science, while speculation belonged to theology. His conclusion that science reveals to us things we can know, while theology only encourages us to believe what we cannot know, clearly separates philosophical thought from Christian thought.[1]

However, not every philosopher distanced himself that far from theology, nor has every theologian moved that far away from philosophy. For example, one of the early Christian thinkers, Saint Augustine of Hippo, argued that philosophical reflections, when firmly rooted in a previous intellectual commitment to the fundamental truth of the Christian faith, complemented theology. Conversely, Tertullian, another early Christian apologist, saw any merger between secular philosophical reasoning with theological reflections as being out of order, claiming that philosophy was the discipline most responsible for heresies.[2]

During the high Middle Ages, Saint Thomas Aquinas expressed that philosophy and theology are distinct enterprises that primarily differ in their intellectual starting points. Philosophy stems from our natural mental faculties with respect to the natural world. On the other hand, theology's starting point is the divine revelations contained in the Bible.[3]

Although a study of philosophy reveals some connection—whether remote or otherwise—to theology, the two will never enjoy a harmonious marriage. Philosophy is, in effect, an effort to address questions about reality and existence, knowledge and reason, and about ethics and language through a critical and systematic approach, and by relying on rational argument. Yet, at its highest level of application, it falls short of supplying the answers for which man seeks and needs.

Philosophy's criticism of religion is that it relies heavily not on empirical evidence, but on faith, seeing it, then, as an exercise with no foundation. For the believer, however, faith does not lack solid footing. Rather, faith rests on the most substantial groundwork of all. That is, it rests on the visible creation, the historical record, the hundreds of witnesses to the bodily resurrection of Jesus Christ, and the accurate fulfillment of biblical prophecy.

Although not all philosophical thought can be considered heretical in relationship to Christianity, and therefore should not be indiscriminately rejected, it becomes so when given equal footing with, or preeminence over, biblical truth. When the wisdom of man is set in opposition to the wisdom of God, philosophy no longer serves pure religion.[4] Since, presumably, philosophy is fundamentally a search for truth and a love of wisdom, when it refuses to accept Christian doctrine as supreme, authoritative, and absolute, it reduces the search to a passing glance.

Of course, the early philosophers did not have the advantage of hearing the teachings of Christ. Their knowledge of Judaism was intellectual, and the prophecies of the coming Messiah had not yet found their fulfillment in His appearance in Bethlehem. Conversely, some of the early church fathers—because of their exposure to the life and ministry of Jesus—took His divinity as establishing the moral authority of earlier biblical writings and, therefore, accepted His teachings as the last word on all things true.

Because of the eternal weight of the message of Jesus Christ, Satan focused his sights on Him and the Christian faith, realizing that, for his evil kingdom to triumph, he had to attack the person and work of God's Son. He knew the best way to do that would be simply to misrepresent Christ, almost imperceptibly making Him an optional component in philosophical reasoning. Satan has always targeted truth and has consistently used distortion to accomplish his evil purpose.

Since the very heart of truth is Jesus Christ himself, "in [whom] dwells all the fullness of the Godhead bodily" (Col.

2:9), discovering truth means discovering the message of the Cross. With all the distortions, revisions, and compromises to truth, that often becomes a formidable undertaking. Jesus Christ—under whose name and upon whose foundation eternal salvation rests—has tragically become relegated to a position no higher than man's own knowledge and no more than equal with other religions of the world.

Some time ago as I sat in my car waiting for a traffic light to change, I noticed a bumper sticker on the car just ahead of me. Although I had seen this same sticker many times and had some idea of its meaning, I had never looked at it long enough to give it much thought. Because of the extended time to scrutinize it, its message became quite clear.

The bumper sticker read, "COEXIST," written with symbols that represented some of the major religious philosophies of the world. The letters formed a crescent moon (representing Islam), a peace symbol, a scientific equation symbol, the star of David, the Wiccan symbol, the Chinese yin-yang symbol, and, finally, a cross (representing Christianity).

Plainly, this popular bumper sticker demonstrates support for religious freedom, tolerance, and understanding. While for many people (even some professing Christians) it all sounds good, a closer look reveals that the various religions of the world that reject Christ are placed on the same level of Christianity. That is, Christianity is just another religion, no better, and perhaps no worse, than any other. The different religious systems now all become equal to the Cross, and in some cases, superior.

In Paul's time, a destructive heretical movement began to take root in Colosse, a movement that struck at the very heart of the Christian faith. Its insidious nature lay in its subtleness. Instead of an outright denial of Christ's legitimacy, the Colossian Christians reduced Him to a station beneath that of the angels, essentially denying His supremacy and sovereignty.

Paul wrote his letter to the Colossians largely to correct the encroachment of this doctrinal error into the ranks of believers. This movement, later referred to as the "Colossian Heresy," and even later developed into full-blown Gnosticism, posed a serious threat to the spiritual life of the church and, consequently, to any serious attempts at Christian service. Knowing he needed to reaffirm truth and restore biblical balance, Paul unmistakably identified Christ as the image of the invisible God, the Creator of all things, and the head of the Church. He left no question that he firmly believed Christ to be divine and supreme, declaring, "That in all things He may have the preeminence" (1:18).

When Paul wrote in Philippians 3:10, "That I may know Him," he spoke of knowledge much different from the knowledge emphasized in Colosse, and much different from the knowledge that is often on display in the religious arena today. Many people throughout the world have *knowledge* of Jesus Christ, but they do not *know* Him personally. Paul's use of the word *knowledge* is not intellectual knowledge but experiential knowledge that springs from God's grace and man's faith. "For by grace you have been saved through faith, and that not of yourselves; it is the gift of God" (Eph. 2:8). Personally knowing Him results in godly character, right attitudes, and proper behavior.

Professing Christians, who only know Christ intellectually, are, in the words of Paul, "enemies of the cross" (Phil. 3:18). That is, they are Christians in theory only, not in practice. They have a philosophy of Christ, but not an experience that affects their character, attitudes, and behavior.

Other distortions of truth surfaced following the time of Christ. Apollinarism, Arianism, Docetism, Sabellianism, and Gnosticism are but a few. These movements, by adding to and taking away from the truth revealed in Jesus Christ, developed religious philosophies detrimental to Christianity. Although religious leaders presented these concepts under the guise of Christianity, a close examination of them reveals that the culprit, again, was philosophy—philosophy mixed with just enough truth to make it appealing, and with just enough error to make it damaging.

Christianity is again being threatened by philosophies that either deny or distort biblical truth. For some years now, the Word of Faith movement has taken unwarranted liberties with God's Word, liberties that especially strike at His sovereignty. Although the stated basis for teaching is Christ, the message quickly moves away from His person, His exemplary life, and His call to radical discipleship. The focus now moves to man and his preoccupation with material, temporary blessings.

The Emergent Church movement, as fundamentally sound in some points as it may be, diverges from certain cardinal truths in a calculated attempt to become more appealing to the surrounding postmodern culture. Leaders in the movement question the Bible's hard-and-fast doctrines and guidelines, opting rather for emphasis on relationship building and mutual acceptance. Their position allows them the flexibility to accept homosexuality, same-sex marriage, premarital sex, and any other behavior that fits into their "relationship building" mold.

Not long ago, I listened to a prominent pastor of a large and thriving evangelical church deliver a message on grace and truth. Interestingly, he spoke as if these expressions of God stood in opposition to each other, voicing that sometimes we have to lay aside truth in order to embrace grace. He appeared to equate *truth* with *judgment*, and *grace* with *forgiveness*. This is confusing, to say the least; and since Christian thought accepts that truth and grace are not two separate doctrines but two facets of a single doctrine, this concept is erroneous. This is another example of emergent-church philosophy that focuses on acceptance at the expense of truth.

We must ask ourselves how these deviations from revealed truth affect biblical Christianity. If we are part of an established conservative evangelical movement, we probably have difficulty imagining how such a significant departure from truth could ever slip through our biblical defenses. Yet, it has happened repeatedly through the centuries, and usually in unsuspecting ways. Doctrinal changes do not occur in a truth-centered church overnight. They happen gradually, and often, along with cultural changes. Like the "frog in the kettle," the changes are so incremental that they go unnoticed until it is too late.

Philosophy in the broader sense—with all its complexities, and with all its direct, or indirect, association with truth—still has to do with man's intellect, and with his observations of life through the rose-colored glasses of mortality. Truth—the acceptance of the Bible as inspired, inerrant, and infallible—stands alone. It needs no propping up and no philosophical concepts to explain.

In placing truth in its proper perspective, Paul wrote, "Let God be true but every man a liar" (Rom. 3:4). That is, we must measure all knowledge against the knowledge of Him who created man in His own image. Any concepts that fall short of this knowledge belong only to the realm of human nature and can never stand the rigorous test of time. If our concepts differ from what "thus says the Lord," then our thoughts will fall to the floor while truth soars on eagles' wings.

5

⊰⌇⊱

Truth Tarnished by Self-Interest

Where do wars and fights come from among you? Do they not come from your desires for pleasure that war in your members? You lust and do not have. . . . You fight and war. Yet you do not have because you do not ask. You ask and do not receive, because you ask amiss, that you may spend it on your pleasures (James 4:1-3).

Over the past few decades, the Christian book market has been flooded with works dealing with physical health, material prosperity, and self-image. Although the Scriptures indeed speak of divine healing, material blessings, and the value of a single person, regrettably, today's emphases on things tangible and temporal have come to dominate the thinking of a certain segment of the Christian community. Many prominent religious personalities have so narrowed their focus to bear on physical and material matters that the broad and encompassing character of the Bible has become lost in a maze of confusion.

Through various religious media—television, radio, seminars, conferences, books, and so on—a precarious imbalance in biblical teaching has grossly distorted sound biblical doctrine. The picture often painted by today's "religious celebrities" is one in which God sits on His throne waiting to receive instructions from us, prepared to quickly rush to our side and grant our every wish. Instead of God creating us for His pleasure, the unspoken sentiment seems to be that He exists for our pleasure.

Unfortunately, many men and women who claim to speak for Christ have shamefully corrupted the Word by making it more about treasures on earth than treasures in heaven, more about physical healing than spiritual healing, and more about the here and now than the hereafter. Many of the supposed "shepherds" of God are in reality "false shepherds," using and abusing the sheep for selfish purposes. Ezekiel 34:2-3 addresses this disturbing reality:

> Son of man, prophesy against the shepherds of Israel, prophesy and say to them, "Thus says the Lord God to the shepherds: 'Woe to the shepherds of Israel who feed themselves! Should not the shepherds feed the flocks? You eat the fat and clothe yourselves with the wool; you slaughter the fatlings, but you do not feed the flock.'"

Amazingly, some of the very ones who claim to speak for God often speak for themselves, fleecing the sheep in the process. These self-appointed shepherds have reduced the Bible to a how-to manual instructing followers on the methods to use to make life on earth more comfortable and gratifying.

Jesus foresaw the day when certain professing Christian leaders would invoke His name to accomplish selfish purposes. He said in His Sermon on the Mount:

Not everyone who says to Me, "Lord, Lord," shall enter the kingdom of heaven, but he who does the will of My Father in heaven. Many will say to Me in that day, "Lord, Lord, have we not prophesied in Your name, cast out demons in Your name, and done many wonders in Your name?" And then I will declare to them, "I never knew you; depart from Me, you who practice lawlessness!" (Matt. 7:21-23).

Notice, Jesus pointed out that these "teachers," on the Day of Judgment, will declare they had done many wonders in *His* name—that is, "in the name of *Jesus.*" It is clear that He was not speaking about politicians, educators, entertainers, or media personalities, because these do not claim to speak in His name. He plainly spoke of religious leaders and teachers. Otherwise, how could they possibly declare that they had done these works in "the name of Jesus"?

These are Ezekiel's shepherds—selfish, uncaring, and materialistic—more concerned about things temporal than things eternal. In spite of what the prosperity teachers assert, Jesus declared:

Do not lay up for yourselves treasures on earth, where moth and rust destroy and where thieves break in and steal; but lay up for yourselves treasures in heaven, where neither moth nor rust destroys and where thieves do not break in and steal. For where your treasure is, there your heart will be also (6:19-21).

There is definite irony to Jesus saying that for some who profess to do good works in His name He would say, "Depart from Me, you who practice lawlessness; I never knew you" (see 7:23). Obviously, simply invoking the name of Jesus means little. It's as if declaring "In the name of Jesus" has some mystical, magical powers that subjects the authority of heaven to man's carnal impulses. That, of course, is simply not true. Nowhere do we find God subjecting His sovereignty to the fleshly desires of self-absorbed people.

Many of today's televangelists imply by their teaching that God's Word emphasizes self-fulfillment above all else. They have systematically redefined Christianity to mean something entirely different from what the Bible says. Whereas God's Word says, "Humble yourselves . . . ," these preachers suggest that we can "elevate ourselves." Although Jesus taught that people who trust in riches cannot enter the kingdom of heaven, these false shepherds declare boldly that God can hardly wait to heap material wealth upon us.

Today's false shepherds use the sheep for their own personal advantage. Furthermore, after they drain from them all they possibly can, they leave them alone in grassless wasteland to fend for themselves. Their unbiblical teaching leads unsuspecting sheep astray.

Professing Christians whose main theme is on the visible and tangible, are foolishly working in opposition to God's Word. Like the ostentatious Pharisees in Matthew 6, they have their reward.

Sometime ago, as I surfed through the television channels—probably looking for a good western—I stopped out of curiosity to listen to such a television preacher, interested in how he used God's Word. I had only been watching for a minute or two when I clearly heard him arrogantly declare, "Truth doesn't change you." Momentarily pausing for effect, he smugly continued, "Repetition changes you."

I must admit, I had never heard that one before. He never explained just what he meant by that statement, and yet the television audience seemed awed by his deep spiritual insight. I suppose that Jesus' saying in John's Gospel, "You shall know the truth, and the truth shall make you free" (8:32), really meant little. This is a good example of how unsuspecting believers are regularly duped by false shepherds.

These false shepherds selectively use the Bible, carefully picking out verses that give credence to their selfish notions, while at the same time conveniently ignoring other portions of Scripture that reveal them for who they really are. It seems apparent by their distortions of God's Word that their foremost interest is self-interest; their focus seems to be on the visible and tangible—prominence, popularity, and the riches of this world. And in the process, they devour and devastate the good of the land, leaving the sheep diseased and disillusioned. The Lord said:

> Is it too little for you to have eaten up the good pasture, that you must tread down with your feet the residue of your pasture—and to have drunk of the clear waters, that you must foul the residue with your feet? And as for My flock, they eat what you have trampled with your feet, and they drink what you have fouled with your feet (Ezek. 34:18-19).

As unconscionable as it is for professing ministers to teach such error, arrogating authority and wealth unto themselves, it is just as unacceptable for students to ignore studying for themselves and refusing to "test the spirits, whether they are of God" (1 John 4:1). Of course, many of these hearers are much like their teachers—usually loving to have their egos stroked, their ears tickled, and their material prosperity assured. Paul's description of this problem to Timothy is a fitting rebuke today:

> Preach the word! Be ready in season and out of season. Convince, rebuke, exhort, with all longsuffering and teaching. For the time will come when they will not endure sound doctrine, but according to their own desires, because they have itching ears, they will heap up for themselves teachers; and will turn their ears away from the truth, and be turned aside to fables (2 Tim. 4:2-4).

False shepherds remain in positions of influence only because students with "itching ears" keep them there. There has always been part of the religious community that only wanted to hear messages of God's bountiful blessings—not ones about responsibility, change, righteousness, or judgment. This self-centered segment continues to create an environment that gives rise to self-seeking shepherds.

Remember the words in James 4:1-3: Seekers fail to receive blessing from God because (1) they do not believe, and (2) they ask for the wrong reasons—that "you may spend it on your own pleasures." One of the reasons the multitudes followed Jesus was because He had fed them with bread and fish. Their interest extended only to their physical and temporal needs. Although some moved from their self-centered interests to a newfound desire to follow Him wholeheartedly, the majority never got beyond the quest to have Jesus only meet their earthly needs.

Clearly, God has not only made provision for our spiritual needs through the sacrifice of Jesus Christ on the cross, He has also provided for our physical and emotional needs. "The chastisement for our peace was upon Him, and by His stripes we are healed" (Isa. 53:5). Paul's words in Philippians 4:19 encompass needs of every description: "And my God shall supply all your need according to His riches in glory by Christ Jesus."

However, nothing in the New Testament indicates that we should place the main emphasis of the Christian life on earthly fulfillment. On the contrary, through searching the Scriptures, we determine the opposite is true—that serving God often means great sacrifice and, sometimes, even means experiencing loss.

When the rich young ruler fell down at Jesus' feet and asked what good thing he could do to inherit eternal life, Jesus answered, "If you want to be perfect, go, sell what you have and give to the poor, and you will have treasure in heaven; and come, follow Me" (Matt. 19:21).

Although committing our lives to Christ is the single most important decision we will ever make, that decision does not exempt us from the often-perilous challenges of living in a world of sin and suffering. In spite of self-interest teaching that suggests we can always have it our way if we only believe, human life is still subject to mortality and to a decaying world. As Job said, "Man who is born of woman is of few days and full of trouble. He comes forth like a flower and fades away; he flees like a shadow and does not continue" (Job 14:1-2).

The enduring promise we have throughout the Christian walk is not that God will lift us up to prominence and wealth in this present life, but that He will "never leave us nor forsake us" (see Heb. 13:5), and that He will elevate us in His time according to His eternal purpose (1 Peter 5:6). This life is not about pleasing ourselves but about pleasing Him who purchased us with His own blood. It is about extending a helping hand to the unsaved; it is about serving the weak and the infirmed, often our own neighbors and acquaintances (Rom. 15:1-2).

In a world immersed in sin—a world where people suffer from spiritual bondage, injustice, disenfranchisement, abuse, loneliness, and hunger—it is inconceivable that ministers of the gospel would spend valuable preaching and teaching time instructing listeners on how to get personal wealth. The logical conclusion is that these supposed shepherds are most concerned about themselves and not about lost and helpless sheep exposed to the elements and to voracious predators.

True spiritual shepherds do not take advantage of God's flock for self-aggrandizement and self-fulfillment. Like Paul, they only boast in the cross of Jesus Christ (Gal. 6:14). Rather, the true servants of our Savior act in accordance to Paul's admonition in Philippians 2:1-4:

> Therefore if there is any consolation in Christ, if any comfort of love, if any fellowship of the Spirit, if any affection and mercy, fulfill my joy by being like-minded, having the same love, being of one accord, of one mind. Let nothing be done through selfish ambition or conceit, but in lowliness of mind let each esteem others better than himself. Let each of you look out not only for his own interests, but also for the interests of others.

Does this sound like God saying to us that our life on earth is about self-interests, prominence, and prosperity? Not quite. The mind of Christ is about serving others; it is about esteeming and inspiring others. Our elevation comes from God in His time and always brings glory to Him.

We can always rest in the truth that our God is constantly working all things together for the ultimate good of His children (Rom. 8:28). Embracing this truth is a distinguishing characteristic of those who have chosen to trust in Him.

If we could somehow create a heaven here in this life, we would never anticipate inhabiting the mansions which Christ departed this earth to prepare for us. He *wants* us to anticipate . . . to look beyond this life . . . to see this world as temporary . . . to know that our life here is a pilgrimage, a journey to a place of unspoiled, eternal splendor.

The hope we have in Christ is a hope that transcends the earthly—the fleshly fulfillment that comes from things transient. John tells us that this world and the covetousness associated with it will one day pass away, but whoever does the will of God will abide forever (1 John 2:17).

As appealing as fame and fortune are, they both pale in comparison to all that God has prepared for those who look for His return. The wealth discovered in Jesus Christ—the wealth of sharing in His glory—is the only lasting wealth. "If indeed we suffer with Him, we [will] also be glorified together. For I consider that the sufferings of this present time are not worthy to be compared with the glory which shall be revealed in us" (Rom. 8:17-18).

On that glorious day when God shall reward His children, the day when the wealth of this world has finally disappeared, the time when the elements have melted with fervent heat, those who have sought to honor and please Him will abide forever as heirs to the Father and joint heirs with Jesus Christ (vv. 16-17).

6

∽જ~

Truth Ignored for the Sake of Promotion

For promotion cometh neither from the east, nor from the west, nor from the south. But God is the judge: he putteth down one, and setteth up another"
(Ps. 75:6-7 KJV).

O ver twenty-five years ago, I arrived at a large denominational conference looking forward to good Christian fellowship as much as all the special events taking place— perhaps even more. This was an important biennial meeting that drew thousands of delegates from around the world. As always, I anticipated seeing friends and fellow ministers whom I only got to see on these special occasions.

When I entered the atrium of the convention center on the first day of the conference, I saw a close friend I had known since our teen years. We had begun in ministry work around the same time, and as a young evangelist, I had preached in his father's church on occasions. He and I shared some memorable times together, establishing a bond that was sure to last a lifetime.

Glad to have found my friend so quickly in such a large gathering, I approached him with the normal delight in seeing a close friend after two years apart. Turning to see me drawing near, he extended his hand to meet my outstretched one.

After a hearty handshake and a brotherly embrace, he ecstatically asked a question that made an unexpected and lasting impression on me. It was not so much that the question was an unusual one; quite the contrary. It was a common one, more expected in the business world, but not unusual in an ecclesiastical system. With an ever-widening grin covering his face, and without the normal exchange of pleasantries, he asked, "Did you hear about my promotion?" His expression was certainly innocent and understandable, and the words that followed conveyed to me that he had landed a highly desirable administrative position in ministry.

Perhaps at that moment, and in my own humanity, I felt a hint of envy, even though I had not sought or desired such a job. At the same time, I felt good for him and offered my congratulations. I never doubted that he had earned such an opportunity, and the years that followed were a testimonial to his work ethic, his love for people, and his leadership ability. Still today, when I observe the ways many church leaders have learned to move deftly within an ecclesiastical system, I come back to this reference to *promotion*.

The question I had then was the very one I have continued to ask over the years. That is, in the context of Christian ministry, what does it really mean to be promoted? I believe that for many ministers, it essentially means the same as in the business world. *Promotion* signifies an appointment or an election to a more prominent and more financially reward-ing position. It means more power and influence. *Promotion*, by definition, means "upward mobility within a particular organization."

The desire for a perceived higher rank is not wrong in it-self. In 1 Timothy 3:1 we read, "If a man desires the position of a bishop, he desires a good work." The "position" here is the office of one with spiritual oversight, at whatever level that may be. Although desire is a fundamental element in pursuing a certain ministry, for that desire to be truly spiritu-al, it must come from the Lord. But is that always the case? Is the desire for a higher ministry office always appropriate?

What, then, does *promotion* in Kingdom work mean? Is it a scriptural concept? If so, does it come from God or man? Does God have a particular service for us to render to Him in a predetermined place for a specific time? On the other hand, does He leave that to His servants to choose?

Some believers interpret every desire in ministry as com-ing from God. Perhaps with some, that may be the case—that is, if those Christian servants have completely brought their flesh under subjection, if they have fully focused their attention on pleasing God, and if they have gotten beyond all debilitating distractions. However, in my sixty-plus years of life, I don't recall ever having met such a person, and I'm surely not one myself. Because of our humanity, and some-times our carnality, we are quite capable of misinterpreting desires. Egos and human emotions often distort the true unfolding of God's plan for His servants.

Christians frequently quote Psalm 37:4 to give weight to the idea that God can hardly wait to satisfy a believer's every desire: "Delight yourself also in the Lord, and He shall give you the desires of your heart." Mistakenly, emphasis is usually placed on the last phrase as opposed to the more important first phrase. Instead of "the desires of your heart," the focus should be on "delight yourself in the Lord." The arrangement of these two phrases expresses the difference between selfish religion and pure religion. If this verse had read, "God will give you the desires of your heart, so delight in Him," the accent would have been on self, which is how many seem to interpret it.[1]

If a believer sincerely seeks to delight in the Lord, then it follows that the servant's desires will intersect with God's will at some point. *Delighting* in Him is about intimacy with Him; it is about serving Him the way He chooses—in His time and in *His* place. Selfish desires fade into insignificance, and the desire to please Him reigns supreme in the life of a true disciple.

Again, what does *promotion* mean in service to God's kingdom? Whatever it may be, or may not be, one thing is certain—proper advancement in ministry comes from the Lord. Regardless of appointments made by ecclesiastical authorities to highly desirable positions, if ultimately such appointments do not fit God's plan, they can never reasonably be considered genuine promotions.

When any person in ministry work asks the question, "Have you heard about my promotion?" the sensible questions to ask in return are, "Why do you call your new job a promotion? Is it because you have more exposure, more influence, and more money, or is it because the Holy Spirit has divinely ordered it? Did the job come through maneuvering, manipulation, and calling in favors, or did it come without any undue pressing of church leaders on your part?"

Having heard this for almost fifty years, I am well aware of how all of it can be explained in the context of God's will. It eases the believer's conscience to embrace the concept that whatever desires in ministry a person has, they presumably come from God. But the fact remains—just because there is a desire for a more conspicuous position, and just because a door may open for such an opportunity, that does not necessarily mean that God has ordered it.

Frequently, I have heard ministers say that if the denomination called upon them through appointment or election to serve in a higher office, they felt a spiritual obligation to do so. The rationale for this thinking usually rests in words such as, "Obey them that have the rule over you [in the Lord]" (Heb. 13:17 KJV). That all sounds good; however, the problem is that many ministers who eagerly accept opportunities to "step up the ladder," considering it the right thing to do, falter when the call is to accept a less prominent job with less pay. The biblical principle of "obeying them that have the rule over you" diminishes considerably when the call does not move in a perceived upward manner. Under those circumstances, the appointment or election is most often seen as a "demotion." That, of course, is the logical conclusion if a minister always sees the higher position as a "promotion."

Under no circumstances do I disparage the elevation of ministers into high offices. That would make absolutely no sense. Any entity consisting of more than a single member needs a leader. And I am confident that God uses the appointive and elective processes to raise up His chosen vessels to fill critical roles in administration and oversight.

It is interesting and quite revealing that some people always denounce ecclesiastical appointments and elections as "political." Of course, that criticism usually comes from the ones not appointed or elected. Amazingly, when those same critics receive appointments to serve in higher offices, the process quickly becomes "spiritual." It only seems to be "political" when it happens to others. When it happens to us, we tend to identify it as God working His will in us.

The problem has never been about elevation and advancement in ministry. Rather, it has always been about motives and methods. God can raise up whomever He chooses, in whatever way He chooses, to fill whatever capacity He chooses. However, when secular principles govern our religious system—wrong motives and manipulation—carnality rules the day. Perceptions of promotion and demotion become motivating, or demoralizing, factors. A sense of value now only comes through the recognition and approval of the denomination. Consequently, certain ministers always make decisions about ministry based on how it may set the stage for an improved position within the organization in the future.

Desirable positions begin to loom large in the viewfinder, often distorting the view of the Kingdom. In whatever manner we may try to justify the actions of working politically within a system to move in a perceived upward motion, God's Word does not support such an action. Consider the following scriptures:

- "So now it was not you who sent me here, but God; and He has made me a father to Pharaoh, and lord of all his house, and a ruler throughout all the land of Egypt" (Gen. 45:8).

- "The Lord makes poor and makes rich; He brings low and lifts up" (1 Sam. 2:7).

- "Thus says the Lord of hosts: 'I took you from the sheepfold, from following the sheep, to be ruler over My people, over Israel'" (2 Sam. 7:8).

- "But God is the Judge: He puts down one, and exalts another" (Ps. 75:7).

- "And He changes the times and the seasons; He removes kings and raises up kings . . ." (Dan. 2:21).

The New Testament follows the same pattern of humility and service. Christ set the perfect example by subjecting Himself to the ultimate "demotion," which we call *condescension.*

Let this mind be in you which was also in Christ Jesus, who, being in the form of God, did not consider it robbery to be equal with God, but made Himself of no reputation, taking the form of a bondservant, and coming in the likeness of men. And being found in appearance as a man,

He humbled Himself and became obedient to the point of death, even the death of the cross. Therefore God also has highly exalted Him . . ." (Phil. 2:5-9).

Is not, indeed, Christ our example? Surely, He is God, and in sacrificing His life, He fulfilled God's eternal purpose. This had to be. Still, Paul makes Christ's perfect submission the pattern for all God's children: "Let this mind be in you which was also in Christ Jesus." This is the mind of Christ, the mind of complete obedience to our Creator. It is His call to order our footsteps, leading us in the path He chooses.

Why, then, do some ministers resort to constant maneuvering and unhealthy overt practices to achieve a desired end? I think we can readily identify some of the answers. For one thing, there are those who feel that validation in ministry only comes through visible advancement. Perhaps their personal insecurities contribute significantly to this mentality, although that offers no excuse. Then, there are those who may have a God-given desire to serve in an important leadership role, but their impatience drives them to force the issue before God's time. Both factors are harmful and, ultimately, obstruct His purpose.

Perceptions, however flawed, eventually become identified as truth. And once that happens, self-serving actions quickly become justifiable. King Saul is a good example of this thought process:

And the people were called together to Saul at Gilgal. . . .

Then he waited seven days, according to the time set by Samuel. But Samuel did not come to Gilgal; and the people were scattered from him. So Saul said, "Bring a burnt offering and peace offerings here to me." And he offered the burnt offering. Now it happened, as soon as he had finished presenting the burnt offering, that Samuel came; and Saul went out to meet him, that he might greet him.

And Samuel said, "What have you done?"

Saul said, "When I saw that the people were scattered from me, and that you did not come within the days appointed, and that the Philistines gathered together at Michmash, then I said, 'The Philistines will now come down on me at Gilgal, and I have not made supplication to the Lord.' Therefore I felt compelled, and offered a burnt offering."

And Samuel said to Saul, "You have done foolishly. You have not kept the commandment of the Lord your God, which He commanded you. For now the Lord would have established your kingdom over Israel forever. But now your kingdom shall not continue" (1 Sam. 13:4, 8-14).

Was it not God's desire that someone offer to Him a burnt offering at this time? Indeed it was. But Saul was not the man. Although, as Israel's king, he had undisputed authority, God had not selected him for this function. In Saul's own mind, he was justified in his actions simply because Samuel failed to show up on time. Later, in chapter 15, he obstinately spared King Agag, because he determined that it was the best action for him to take. Although Samuel commanded

Saul to destroy not only Agag but also every living creature of the Amalekites, he rebelliously returned with the pagan king and the finest of the sheep and oxen, ostensibly to offer sacrifices to God.

Saul perceived that all of his actions were justified, having selfishly superimposed his will over God's will. Are not some church leaders often guilty of the same thought processes, overlooking the notion that perhaps God has a better plan? Self-seeking, egocentric motives always make man's designs look more appealing than God's plan, while at the same time, attributing every whimsical desire to God.

We cannot afford to jeopardize the Lord's work by arrogantly adjusting His will to fit our personal plans and ambitions. The challenge, of course, is to walk closely enough to God to be able to discern the difference between what we want and what He wants.

The Lord said to Moses, "And if you make Me an altar of stone, you shall not build it of hewn stone; for if you use your tool on it, you have profaned it" (Ex. 20:25).

Anything beyond the plain and simple untouched stone would only have polluted the altar. Supporting this truth is the principle of God's appointed way. Any attempt to improve on His way is to inject human nature into an arena where angels fear to tread. Intruding into God's jealously guarded domain, into His realm of hidden secrets—however well-intended—is to pollute the very thing that God has called *sacred*.[2]

God's altar is an expression of His will. If we try to improve it, then it becomes an expression of our will—in essence, an altar of self. Whatever sacrifice a worshiper offers upon this altar indeed may bring some measure of emotional satisfaction, but under no circumstances can it ever satisfy a holy God.

In our worship and service, God requires essentially two things, both involving a reasonable measure of self-control: *humility* and *reverence*. This fixes the heart on God, and when that happens, no place is left for self. Promotion takes on an entirely different meaning. That is, wherever God's will takes us must be considered a promotion, meaning that every time we answer God's call, He elevates us. For example, if God calls a certain pastor to resign a larger church to accept a much smaller pastorate, we can be sure that, if he accepts the call, God lifts him up. Obviously, this concept is diametrically opposed to the world's view, but this is the remarkable difference between the spiritual and the natural.

Anytime a servant of the Lord opts to leave a ministry to which God has appointed him or her in order to secure a supposed higher position, in reality, that person's change in status is not an honest promotion. Stepping outside of God's perfect will may bring some immediate recognition and benefits, but over time, it hampers God's work.

Paul cautioned, "Therefore do not be unwise, but understand what the will of the Lord is" (Eph. 5:17). It's not that God's will is hard to understand, but rather, that it's not always easy to accept. For a child of God to desire a particular ministry office—pastoral, administrative, or otherwise—is not in itself wrong. Again, the all-important question is about motives: What is the driving force behind a minister seeking a certain office? If it is indeed a burning desire to fulfill God's will, then the servant should seek *Him* and not the *office*.

When Christ said, "Seek first the kingdom of God and His righteousness, and all these things shall be added to you" (Matt. 6:33), His words extended to every portion of our lives. In the realm of Christian service, improper motives lead people to seek *ministries* more than *Jesus*. If we seek the person of Jesus Christ with our whole hearts, there is no reason to doubt He will judiciously direct our footsteps along the path of His choosing.

It must be His kingdom we seek to build, not our own. Nothing we build in our own name and through our own power will last. Unless we build on the solid rock of Jesus Christ, submitting to His perfect will, our building will not be substantial. "And the rain descended, the floods came, and the winds blew and beat on that house; and it fell . . ." (Matt. 7:27).

As mentioned earlier in the chapter, Paul wrote that if a man "desires the position [office] of a bishop, he desires a good work." He prefaced his words with, "This is a faithful saying" (1 Tim. 3:1), meaning that the saying was known and truthful. Paul now makes it clear that such an office is not for everyone, that it's not merely a title of honor or a position of power, but rather a strenuous office—an office with a supreme regard for God's glory and man's benefit. After writing of the desire, Paul follows with the demanding regulations placed on a person with such a desire:

> A bishop then must be blameless, the husband of one wife, temperate, sober-minded, of good behavior, hospitable, able to teach; not given to wine, not violent, not greedy for money, but gentle, not quarrelsome, not covetous; one who rules his own house well, having his children in submission with all reverence (for if a man does not know how to rule his own house, how will he take care of the church of God?); not a novice, lest being puffed up with pride he fall into the same condemnation as the devil. Moreover he must have a good testimony among those who are outside, lest he fall into reproach and the snare of the devil (vv. 2-7).

God said to Isaiah, "For My thoughts are not your thoughts, nor are your ways My ways. . . . For as the heavens are higher than the earth, so are My ways higher than your ways, and My thoughts than your thoughts" (55:8-9). The calling is God's calling, the ministry is His ministry, and the offices are His offices. We are but bondservants that He has so honored by His holy calling. How He calls, and to what kind of ministry He calls, is strictly according to His choosing. Any foolish attempt to circumvent His guidelines, and any effort to revise His Word to accommodate selfish desires and motives, will eventually meet with failure.

Promotion . . . what is it? True promotion, the kind that comes from God himself, always means following the leadership of His Holy Spirit in order to accomplish His will, even when that means giving up prominent leadership roles and highly desirable offices to serve without recognition and honor from man. Thankfully, many have chosen that path, believing that the work of the Lord is a work worthy of the highest level of unselfish and sacrificial labor. In the process, these often-unheralded ministers and Christian servants have found unspeakable fulfillment, peace of mind, and a Word-centered anticipation of heaven's reward for faithfulness.

7

⟳⟳

Truth Obscured
by Marketing Techniques

*Woe to those who go down to Egypt for help, and rely
on horses, who trust in chariots because they are many,
and in horsemen because they are very strong, but who
do not look to the Holy One of Israel, nor seek the Lord!*
(Isa. 31:1).

Whatever the general public interprets the Christian
movement to be or not to be, we must necessarily
conclude that, at the very least, it is the ultimate faith-based
operation. Even though good business practices are necessary, proper structure is essential, and publicity is indispensable, the body of Christ must operate, first, on faith in its
Founder and, second, on the highest level of integrity and
accountability.

Living in the greatest capitalistic society in the history of
man, we have learned the value of marketing. Goods not only
have to be produced, they have to be distributed and sold,
hopefully to an eager public. In such a free market environment, a money system, entrepreneurialism, and competition
are necessary components, ideally engendering healthy business practices, maximum production, and appealing marketing

techniques. Capitalism cannot survive without the constant interaction of these, and other, significant elements.

Our economic system has become so much part of us until we apply its principles to virtually every part of our lives. For example, consider child rearing—teaching children the value of a dollar, the benefit of producing and saving, and the principle of performance and reward. In this same spirit, churches work hard to maximize their effectiveness in their respective communities. And to do that, churches have to implement a certain amount of planning, organization, promotion, and publicity.

To believe it is unbiblical for a church to use effective marketing strategies to further its purpose is unfounded supposition. Although in the past few years an abundance of literature opposing the "marketing" of the church has been published, nowhere in Scripture do we find prohibitions against promoting and publicizing the local church and its ministries.

Progressive churches regularly use surveys to determine the application of methods suitable to a given community of believers, and suitable to the geographical community surrounding them. Often, such surveys focus on worship styles, music preferences, interaction opportunities, family-oriented ministries, support groups, and relevant preaching. These churches then develop strategies to connect with the expressed needs in its communities. Often, these needs are considered "felt needs" and, in the minds of some, fit into the seeker-friendly, or seeker-sensitive, framework.

In addition to researching worship preferences in a given location, growing churches study the demographics of a particular community, utilize bulk mailings, advertise via the Internet, and develop informational, easy-to-use, and eye-catching websites. These cutting-edge churches employ a wide variety of marketing strategies to get the attention of unchurched people, and work hard to hone their techniques, not wanting to overlook a practical plan for effective outreach.

Ministers and church leaders who criticize principles of marketing could very well have more trouble with the term itself than with its actual function. The term *marketing* tends to have a negative connotation in the realm of something as spiritual as Christianity and the religious community. Consequently, some ministers cringe at the thought of merging into one common thread the "gospel" and "marketing."

Of course, we don't have to look very long and hard to find churches whose marketing practices are highly questionable. For instance, there are churches whose marketing plans give unwarranted consideration to newcomers by reducing the emphasis on the parts of God's Word that deal with personal responsibility and judgment. That is, they try to make the church experience more palatable to the public by ignoring Christian duty and by choosing not to mention sin and its consequences.

Again, to some believers, these two terms—*gospel* and *marketing*—are incompatible. Is not the gospel disseminated by the operation of the Holy Spirit through Christ's followers, and are not sinners convicted of sins by the same divine power? Why is it, then, that we feel the need to utilize modern advertising and marketing methods? By resorting to these means of promoting the church, its missions, and its ministries, are we depending more on the arm of the flesh and human resources than we are on the supernatural action of God himself?

We must answer these questions objectively and conscientiously. To do so appropriately, we have to take a panoramic view of God's plan of eternal redemption, considering the human element as well as the divine function. Since God chose man as His vessel of service, both sides in the equation are vital. God provides the truth, the instructions, and the divine power, while man brings to the table a yielded instrument, an obedient heart, and an acceptable human methodology. The challenge for believers is to utilize the best methods to disseminate the gospel and to make disciples without compromising the truth.

Some years ago, I recall listening to a motivational speaker, who also served as the pastor of a large and highly visible church, being interviewed by a prominent television talk-show host. When the host asked this avowed evangelical minister about the necessity of being *born again,* the pastor sadly sidestepped the issue, never stating publicly that he believed it was an absolute necessity for everyone. He only emphasized that he believed such an experience was important for *him*.

Was this minister's concern about sounding too offensive before a large television audience justified? Perhaps. Should he have given a more direct answer on a subject as eternal as the new birth? Absolutely.

Although I believe that being evasive when asked about God's plan of salvation is unacceptable, adjusting the presentation of the gospel message to connect with a particular audience, or a particular culture, is not, in itself, wrong. The apostle Paul made it clear that he felt constrained to do just that in order to communicate the truth revealed in Jesus Christ. He wrote:

> For though I am free from all men, I have made myself a servant to all, that I might win the more; and to the Jews I became as a Jew, that I might win Jews; to those who are under the law, as under the law, that I might win those who are under the law; to those who are without law, as without law (not being without law toward God, but under law toward Christ), that I might win those who are without law; to the weak I became as weak, that I might win the weak. I have become all things to all men, that I might by all means save some (1 Cor. 9:19-22).

Whether church-related or otherwise, a particular audience determines some elements of communication. If communication becomes complete, not only must someone deliver a message, but someone has to understand and receive it. No one understood this principle better than Jesus did.

Consequently, He communicated truth in a manner that thoughtfully touched on various elements of His culture. He gathered around Him disciples whom He organized and sent out by twos to reach the lost sheep of Israel; He developed parables to convey the issues of life effectively; and He audaciously broke with Jewish tradition, foregoing the ceremonial washing of His hands, to sit at a table with sinners.

Every generation has used marketing strategies common to its day in order to attract attention to the church and its message. Because societies constantly change through education, economics, and philosophy, the church must necessarily adjust its methods in order to communicate the message that Jesus Christ is still the Savior of the world. Therefore, the problem is not so much "marketing" but, rather, understanding the role of the human element of marketing in the effort to enlarge the spiritual kingdom of our Lord.

As in other parts of this writing, the watchword is *balance.* As important as good marketing practices are, they must never be an end in themselves. That is, they cannot stand alone, and they must never obscure biblical truth. In fact, church marketing strategies often take precedence over the proclamation of the gospel. In such cases, church becomes more about human celebrity, expertise, creativity, and man's ability to maintain what often becomes little more than an attractive social and political institution.

Growing up in a full-gospel evangelical church, I have often heard it said that God doesn't anoint programs, He anoints people. I believe that to be a true statement. Redeemed and Spirit-filled people are His chosen and anointed vessels. Highly organized programs, well-structured systems, and imaginative advertising strategies may be good and useful, but the Holy Spirit does not settle upon these things. He settles upon His people, empowering them to reach the harvest, to heal the hurting, to strengthen the weak, and to lift up the downtrodden. In the words of Zechariah, it is " 'Not by might, nor by power, but by My Spirit,' says the Lord of hosts" (4:6).

As important as it is to apply good business principles and practices to the operation of the local church, to make use of marketing strategies not in conflict with Scripture, and to present the best image possible in the community, the church remains the quintessential faith-based organization. That is, with all the above, unless we, as members of the body of Christ, are receiving our instructions from God's Word, are staying close to God through spiritual praying and worship, and are receiving empowerment from the Holy Spirit to serve, ours is an exercise in futility.

Marketing techniques, however beneficial, do not stand alone. Without the driving force of truth, all the sophisticated marketing strategies in the world become nothing more than attractive window dressings, creating outward appeal but having no power to address the deep spiritual needs of a declining culture. A nation drowning in moral depravity desperately cries out for a church that is firmly and uncompromisingly grounded in truth, not one preoccupied with material publicity and image.

Ultimately, creative marketing methods may accomplish some things, but not the main thing, which is the proclamation that salvation only comes through Jesus. In spite of the fact that the Christian church in America soft-pedals this message with increasing frequency—for one reason, to appear less offensive—the apostle Paul's words still ring clear: "For no other foundation can anyone lay than that which is laid, which is Jesus Christ" (1 Cor. 3:11).

The very best marketing technique for the church is one that has nothing to do with professional advertisement, highly organized programs, or clever image building. It rather has to do with the personal testimonies of people whose lives have been genuinely changed by the power of the gospel of Jesus Christ. Nothing attracts sincere seekers to a given church like the witness of those who, like Paul, have experienced becoming a new creation in Christ—old things having passed away, and all things becoming new (2 Cor. 5:17).

The woman of Samaria, after encountering Christ, returned to the city and declared, "Come, see a Man who told me all things that I ever did. Could this be the Christ?" (John 4:29).

Scripture continues, "And many of the Samaritans of that city believed in Him because of the word of the woman who testified . . ." (v. 39). The people of the city responded, "Now we believe . . . for we ourselves have heard Him and we know that this is indeed the Christ, the Savior of the world" (v. 42).

Absolutely nothing can ever take the place of the simple preaching and teaching of God's Word, for the effectiveness of truth rests, not in man's strategies, but in the prevailing and convincing work of the Holy Spirit.

8

෯෯

Truth Subject to Creative Thinking

And we have such trust through Christ toward God.
Not that we are sufficient of ourselves to think of anything
as being from ourselves, but our sufficiency is from God
(2 Cor. 3:4-5).

Imagination is a wonderful thing. It can transport a child into the distant past to sit at King Arthur's Round Table, to far-flung planets in the present era, and to a futuristic world controlled by androids. Imagination provides the groundwork upon which to erect splendid skyscrapers, create majestic theme parks, and build prolific empires of industry. As intangible as dreams are in their infancy, they are nonetheless an integral part of developing socially and psychologically, and indeed become the springboard for incredible accomplishments.

Libraries of books have been written about the human mind—its power, its resourcefulness, and its complexities and mysteriousness. On the one hand, the mind is inclined to contemplate the existence of a Supreme Being; on the other hand, it is capable of desperately wicked thoughts. Man's mind can be creative and flexible, given both to rational and irrational considerations. Its power can control, motivate, influence, and manipulate the masses. The unchained mind is so powerful that God spoke concerning the building of Babel, "Indeed the people are one and they all have one language, and this is what they begin to do; now nothing that they propose to do will be withheld from them" (Gen. 11:6).

Because of the power and influence of the mind, it is extremely important to think right thoughts and to speak right words. Norman Vincent Peale influenced millions of people with his emphasis on *The Power of Positive Thinking*. His words were uplifting and inspirational, conveying to readers and listeners alike the potency of a positive mental attitude. Peale understood that maintaining the right state of mind counterbalanced the human tendency to murmur, grumble, and complain. He was keenly aware that right thinking properly set the tone for meaningful interaction with superiors, subordinates, and peers.

There is, however, a sharp dividing line between all that relates to positive thinking, which occurs in the natural realm, and all that references biblical faith, which occurs in the spiritual realm. The problem is not positive thinking but, rather, that a positive mental attitude is often confused with faith. Although both mental and spiritual exercises are important to physical, psychological, and spiritual health, only faith genuinely connects us to God.

As useful as positive thinking is, we must understand that it focuses on *us*—that is, it depends on what we can do for ourselves. Conversely, faith looks beyond us to focus on its indispensable object, Jesus Christ. Therefore, a positive mental attitude concentrates on what we can do through our own imagination and strength, while faith embraces what God can do in our behalf through His perfect knowledge and grace.

Since the fall of man in Eden, the human mind has always been the Enemy's battleground. From the time the serpent tempted Eve in Genesis 3:4-5 to doubt God's word by declaring, "You will not surely die," man has grappled with Satan's influences upon his mind. Those influences come in different forms, often in the form of an inflated sense of self. And that undue appraisal of self and dependence on the power of man's mind is usually the very thing that distorts truth in a most subtle manner.

Man is a tripartite being—spirit, soul, and body—and since the soul is the seat of the emotions, the will, and the personality, it mirrors the influences of the mind. Consequently, the Bible has much to say about man's thinking:

- "The Lord searches all hearts and understands all the intents of the thoughts" (1 Chron. 28:9).

- "The righteous God tests the hearts and minds" (Ps. 7:9).

- "The Lord knows the thoughts of man" (94:11).

- "Thus says the Lord . . . I know the things that come into your mind [every one of them]" (Ezek. 11:5).

- "Jesus knew their thoughts" (Matt. 12:25).

Clearly, the way we think is important. Our thoughts reflect who we are and what we believe; and more than likely, they will, at some point, be expressed verbally. Because the mind is the gateway into the heart and soul of man, Satan gives special attention to influencing our thoughts.

Disturbingly, many of today's Christian leaders frequently emphasize dreaming and imagining for big things more than they do calling on believers to pray and trust God to work *His* will. Man's capacity to dream big dreams is often cited more than God's contribution to improving the human condition. There appears to be an unspoken sentiment that believers need to develop a dream and then appeal to God for His participation. That all may sound good, but there is a distinct line that separates ideas generated within the mind from those produced within the spirit through God's revealed and spoken Word.

Granted, sometimes mental pictures, or imaginations, are the result of God's impressions upon man's heart. If so, then it follows that the dream filling a person's mind is one actually birthed in the heart as a direct result of the interaction between the sovereign God and spiritual faith. The danger is that we often want something so badly that we carelessly superimpose our dreams of success over God's perfect will.

Creative thinking for the believer—however valuable it may be—is not always the product of divine authorship or leadership, although it may be. Often, the capacity to envision a particular objective evolves from personal interests erroneously interpreted as visions from God. This exercise is frequently trumpeted more in the context of corporate America's business model—dreaming, strategizing, promoting, and marketing—than in the realm of God's spiritual kingdom. In this context, the ability of the human mind to creatively think becomes the catalyst to receive God's blessings and favor, as opposed to applying biblical faith.

As inventive and ingenious as the mind of man is, it is still an imperfect instrument—weak, restricted, and carnal. Just as we cannot do enough good works to justify ourselves before God, neither can we dream enough to build great churches or to minister to the masses. The work of God's kingdom will never be accomplished through the dreams and imaginations of men.

Having served in ministry more than forty-four years—over thirty of those years in pastoral ministry—I have attended countless church conferences and seminars. As helpful as most of those conferences were, I was frequently disengaged because I lacked a familiar point of reference. Although I always enjoyed hearing the remarkable success stories, especially coming from noted pastors of large and thriving churches, I had difficulty connecting with those stories because my world of pastoral ministry was nothing like the ones described. I departed from some of those conferences more disheartened than motivated. Occasionally, the emphasis in those meetings seemed to be more on man as the facilitator of growth and change instead of the Lord. Neither was it unusual to hear the business model referenced as the pattern for personal enrichment and church growth.

Often, pastors of average-size churches or smaller are made to feel less than successful, out of touch, or simply not imaginative enough when they are pressed to compare themselves to highly successful pastors of megachurches. It is also possible for sincere servants of the Lord to dream past their gifts and callings, and when those things imagined do not come to pass, they are left with only feelings of frustration and failure. In fact, not every church leader or pastor is called to lead a superministry or pastor a large multifaceted church.

Regardless of big dreams and innovations in ministry, Psalm 127:1 still declares, "Unless the Lord builds the house, they labor in vain who build it." God's Word has never defined success in ministry in terms of results, but rather in terms of obedience, trust, and faithfulness. Results rest in His hands.

It is deeply troubling to think that perhaps only those who are highly imaginative, those who are prone to dreaming big, and those who are naturally given to deep contemplation are the ones most successful in the Lord's work. However, if we follow the business model, that's the assumption we make. What that essentially means is that any person's inability to dream big is in reality a hindrance to God working in and through that person. Biblical faith is now replaced by the capacity and power of man's mind.

Church leaders who leave the impression that dreaming, or visualizing, is so vital to spiritual health should speak of dreams and imaginations in the context of spiritual faith. And I am confident that many do. However, if that is indeed true, those leaders should seriously consider adjusting their words in order to forestall any confusion over what often appears as an undue emphasis on the power and creativity of the human mind.

Interestingly, out of thirty-six references in the King James Version of the Bible to some form of the words *imagine* and *imagination*, thirty-five of those verses either directly reference, or imply, evil and selfish thoughts—the only exception being 1 Chronicles 29:18. Further, the references to *dreams* deal with thoughts that come, either miraculously or naturally, while a person is in a state of sleep. Those dreams have nothing to do with creative thinking. If the Bible is our guide, and it most certainly is, then we must carefully present the truth as it is contained therein and refrain from building a Christian philosophy on concepts that, in the context of Scripture, stand in opposition to truth.

The all-important question is, "What really are we communicating?" In today's culture, the frequent references to *dreaming big* and *imagining what we can be* usually rest on the power and influence of the mind. When the same language is used in the Christian movement, the implication is basically the same and often sends conflicting signals, whether innocently or by design.

Here is another question we are sorely pressed to answer: "Is it our ability to dream that prompts God's favor, or is it

God's willingness to work in our behalf based on His will and our simple faith in Him—*faith as a grain of mustard seed*?"

The thought that any believer lacking imagination and mentally incapable of dreaming big dreams will be penalized by God is inconceivable. There is not a single Scripture reference that would lead us to come to such a conclusion. The very idea that spiritual faith is merely the assent of the mind to a divine revelation is foreign to God's Word.

Although faith may inspire dreams and imaginations, faith is the God-given capacity to inwardly trust *Him*. Although there is much we can do to develop faith, there is nothing we can do within ourselves to acquire it; it is a gift of God. "For I say, through the grace given to me, to everyone who is among you, not to think of himself more highly than he ought to think, but to think soberly, as God has dealt to each one a measure of faith" (Rom. 12:3).

Maintaining a positive mental attitude, speaking words of affirmation, and envisioning bigger and better things are beneficial exercises, but they are not substitutes for true faith in Jesus Christ. There is the ever-present danger that the dividing line between the natural and the spiritual will become blurred, giving rise to dependence on human ability in order to obtain spiritual blessings.

Our walk with Christ is not a walk of seeing, feeling, and dreaming. Neither is it a walk enhanced by the power of man's imagination. Rather, it is a walk of *genuine faith*—the kind of faith that is not as much about seeing, hearing, or believing God for a particular answer as it is about simply believing that He is God, that He exists in majesty and glory, that He is all-powerful, that He is full of grace and truth, and that He is always acting in the best interest of His children. It is believing that He is always working for our ultimate good and that His purposes are far beyond what our eyes can see, beyond what our hands can feel, and beyond what our minds can dream and imagine.

In reality, mental power does not necessarily increase possibilities in the work of God's kingdom, but often only hinders God's supernatural work. When Paul wrote, "But God has chosen the foolish things of the world to put to shame the wise, and God has chosen the weak things of the world to put to shame the things which are mighty" (1 Cor. 1:27), he understood that the very best efforts of any human being would so pale in comparison to the mightiness of God that those efforts would hardly be worth mentioning. It is only when we operate outside ourselves, outside the limitations of our personal dreams and ideas, and begin to operate in the realm of the spiritual, directed and empowered by the Holy Spirit, that we truly expand the kingdom of heaven.

Our only lasting accomplishments are those done, not in our own power and might, but instead by the power of His Spirit. It is not that dreaming, or visualizing (getting a mental picture of what we would like to achieve in the ministry

God has called us to) is a wrong and unhealthy exercise. It only becomes unhealthy when we attempt to use *our* dreams and *our* visions to influence God to accomplish through us what *we* choose. On the other hand, if we are first influenced by truth, if we operate through faith in God's Word, then it stands to reason that our trust in Him will, in some measure, translate to envisioning what He can do through us.

As in every work God calls us to do, we must conscientiously follow the leadership of the Holy Spirit, doing all in the name of Jesus and for His glory alone. In nothing we do for Him should we be ashamed—nor in anything we do for Him should we glory.

Ultimately, we are responsible to direct attention *away* from us, *away* from our God-given abilities and expertise, *away* from our knowledge and skills, and direct all attention to *Him* in whose hands rest all power and might. We must remember:

- We're the clay; He's the Potter.

- We're the servants; He's the Master.

- We're the building; He's the Builder.

- We're unwise; He's all-wise.

- We're imperfect; He's perfect.

- We're unknowing; He's all-knowing.

- We're weak and trembling; He's strong and stable.

- We're full of selfishness and stubbornness; He's full of grace and mercy.

- We're frail and lowly human beings; He's the exalted Lord of Glory, the Almighty God—the only Being with true creative thoughts.

9

⚜

Truth Diluted by Liberal Religious Education

*Having a form of godliness but denying its power.
And from such people turn away! . . . Always learning
and never able to come to the knowledge of the truth*
(2 Tim. 3:5, 7).

If history teaches us anything, it teaches us that change, whether favorable or unfavorable, occurs gradually. Deteriorating relations among nations do not happen overnight; the rise of democracies, or dictatorships, does not come about with a single election; economic systems, however simple or complex, do not rise and fall on one solitary policy. Neither do religious denominations become bastions of liberal thought with the influence of a lone voice of compromise. Just as time can be the friend of a growing Christian consciousness, it can also be the enemy of conservative religious thought.

For anyone seriously seeking the truth about the deeply religious founding of America, there lie undeniable proofs in every direction. A person only has to read America's unbiased history to discover that its founders determined it would be a nation established upon the Christian faith and Christian principles.

The oldest institution of higher learning in the United States, Harvard, began in 1636 as a training ground for Christian ministers. The same can be said about almost all other colleges during early America. Of the first 108 such schools, approximately 106 were established as Christian institutions. In fact, the roots of today's public school system rest in the determination of our founders to provide our young nation's children with the tools to read and understand the Bible, and to learn to properly apply its principles in daily life.

How is it, then, that education in the United States, both public and private, has drifted so far from its origins? How have we not only divorced Christian education from the public forum, but also have arrogantly and systematically removed the teaching of cardinal truths from religious institutions? As hard as it is to understand how we as a nation have so distanced ourselves from our Christian underpinnings, it is even more difficult to understand how our religious movements have distanced themselves from the very heart of truth, Jesus Christ.

Indeed, the pursuit of education is a worthy and lifelong process. Whether occurring naturally through living and maturing, or through a well-developed system of focused instruction, the quest for education at any level is commendable and obtaining it is admirable.

Regardless of the level of learning reached, most people would likely admit a desire for more education, not less.

Whatever a person learns in life, there is always another reality to discover, another area of knowledge to acquire, and additional information to access. The rapid advance of technology and the more specialization in the workplace demand a higher level of practical knowledge and increased proficiency in performance.

One area where we have seen a significant increase in candidates for graduate-level education is in the field of Christian ministry. More and more ministerial students are completing master's and doctoral programs; some denominations, of course, require these degrees, but not all. Accessing education today is much easier than ever before. Continuing education programs, satellite campuses, and online colleges bring the education experience much closer home—and they do it more economically.

Consider these thought-provoking questions regarding education for students in the field of Christian ministry: Is higher education what it is touted to be? Is it for everyone? Should it be a prerequisite for ministerial status within a given denomination?

Obviously, not all religious organizations answer these questions in the same manner. Still, even those denominations that heretofore have had few expectations relating to formal degrees are moving closer to having their ministerial candidates meet more stringent formal education requirements. Clearly, this follows the secular model, which demands a higher level of formal training because of increasing emphasis on specialization.

Interestingly, the Amish community only allows its children to complete eight grades of formal schooling. Among the reasons for their limited approach to formal instruction is a belief that any education beyond the eighth grade only engenders pride. Until a landmark decision by the United States Supreme Court on May 15, 1972, much controversy surrounded this concept. Essentially, the high court ruled that the Amish have the right to maintain a community-based Amish education for their students by exempting them from compulsory attendance laws beyond the eighth grade. The court based its decision on the grounds that a conventional formal education provided by a certified high school interferes with the child's adolescent period of religious development.

The Amish remain firm in their objection to high school and college education. They continue to believe that by limiting exposure to unconventional ideas and by limiting social contact with students outside their community, their narrowly focused education system preserves the traditions and values of their culture and discourages the young adult from leaving the Amish community.

Are we to laud the Amish for their concerns about pride and for their ability to keep their community together virtually crime-free? Indeed, we are. Do we need to embrace a similar education system for our culture, hoping to return to a more pastoral life? Probably not. What works for them would not necessarily work for people outside their community. As a nation, we cannot turn the clock back to a time that once was—that is, to an agrarian, largely immobile, society. We have now become too urban and suburban for that. Most of us live within a technologically advancing community that dictates we adjust in order to compete in the marketplace.

Still, a college education, secular or religious, is not for everyone. But for Christians suited for it, the challenge is to strike the delicate balance between advancing academically and retaining biblically conservative ideas in the process. As uncomplicated as that seems to be, it is not always the case.

The Bible frequently affirms those who seek knowledge, although the knowledge referenced generally has to do with God. Consider these verses:

- "Receive my instruction, and not silver, and knowledge rather than choice gold" (Prov. 8:10).

- "Wise people store up knowledge" (10:14).

- "A man of knowledge increases strength" (24:5).

- "Add to your faith virtue, to virtue knowledge" (2 Peter 1:5).

The Scripture also has something to say about knowledge that becomes an end in itself:

- "He who increases knowledge increases sorrow" (Eccl. 1:18).

- "Knowledge puffs up, but love edifies" (1 Cor. 8:1).

These Scripture references lead us to conclude there exists a tension between spiritual knowledge and secular knowledge. This clash does not necessarily suggest worldly knowledge is harmful or prohibited. What it does suggest, however, is that we measure any knowledge acquired against an all-knowing, all-wise, all-powerful, and self-existent God, and submit such knowledge to His eternal truths.

Unfortunately, higher education, whether in liberal arts or religion, tends to question long-held beliefs about God and His plan of salvation. Clearly, when a professor in a secular university challenges the Christian worldview, no one should be surprised. However, when a seminary professor challenges established Christian beliefs, everyone should be troubled.

Why would a Christian college or seminary chip away at the very foundation of its existence? Is it conceivable that such an institution would systematically attack creationism, the deity and resurrection of Jesus, and other essential declarations in Scripture? When religious institutions jettison long-held beliefs about Christ and Christianity, the reasonable assumption is that such an institution would drop all association and identification with the Christian faith. However, that's not what usually follows. Apparently, it is not enough for some religious educational institutions to reject the infallibility of the Bible, they often seem determined to radically alter the face of biblical Christianity.

An example of the evolving liberal view of religious education in America can be seen in Claremont Seminary in

California, founded in 1885 by Charles Maclay, a Methodist minister and state senator. After a long trend toward liberal religious philosophy, more recently it determined to move in an even more inclusive direction. This once Christian college reportedly has now become the first seminary in the United States to become a multifaith institution.

Intent on embracing the growing diversity of America's religious landscape, the Claremont School of Theology, in 2010, added clerical training for Muslims and Jews to its curriculum and has announced that it hopes to offer training for Buddhists and Hindus in the future. In fairness to the United Methodist Church, which has provided a percentage of the school's annual budget, this decision by Claremont has strained relations between the school and more conservative elements within the denominational body.[1]

Liberal religious thought is not new in America. Although it has shown up in all periods of our history, it most notably influenced American culture between 1870 and 1970. During this time, it has had a serious debilitating effect on the evangelical Christian movement.

Even though many reasons exist for such a seismic shift in religion's point of reference, one of the most significant ones is that prominent and socially acceptable seminaries felt compelled to employ a liberal interpretation of the Bible as a rational response to the fervent evangelicalism that permeated most denominations during that era. In essence, the intellectual challenges of Darwinism and higher biblical criticism—challenges that had been stirring in academia since the middle of the nineteenth century—led religious educators to challenge biblical authenticity, virtually eliminating any reference to the supernatural from the vocabulary of biblical scholars.[2]

These powerful educational influences had a major impact on mainline Protestant churches during the time frame mentioned. To understand better how formal religious training changed the meaning of Christianity, we only have to look at the modifications made in mainline denominations since the early establishment of their colleges and universities.

For example, during the past two and a half centuries since the birth of the Methodism—a movement resulting from John Wesley's efforts to revive the Anglican Church—this once conservative, revivalist movement faced monumental challenges within its ranks. Although initially holding to a literal interpretation of Scripture and to New Testament revivalism and evangelism, as time passed, it began struggling against a growing faction on the inside that embraced truth as relative.

In the early 1800s, when many pioneers left their homes and churches in the East to settle in the American West, a Methodist minister, Francis Asbury (1745-1816), followed along. Circuit-riding preachers spreading the gospel of Jesus Christ were a hallmark of the Methodist movement, and English-born Asbury was one of them.

Francis Asbury roamed the American wilderness for forty years, planting the seeds of Jesus Christ everywhere he traveled. He faced the dangers of Indian attacks, bitter cold winters, and deprivations that would have defeated lesser men. In the process, he quite possibly covered more than 250,000 miles in a land without roads, and preached perhaps 25,000 sermons. Asbury's determined and untiring leadership helped spread Methodism in America.

By the close of the 1700s, God powerfully moved in the newly constituted nation in what we now refer to as the Second Great Awakening. During this time, the Christian movement in America experienced the birth of the camp meetings, generally believed to have begun in Kentucky's Logan County. In the forefront of this marvelous outpouring of God's Spirit, we find the Methodist. Although this revival movement reached across denominational lines, the normally accepted historical record places the Methodist in a foundational role of this spiritual awakening—an awakening that proved to be the roots of the Pentecostal Movement in the latter half of the 1800s and early 1900s.

Something happened to reverse the revival trend set in motion by men like John Wesley and George Whitefield. Even though mainline churches, especially the Methodists, had powerfully influenced people with the profound gospel of Jesus Christ and had called, perhaps, two generations of believers to a life of holiness, that now began to change.

Through their many colleges and seminaries, these denominations began calling in question a literal interpretation of the Bible, the significance of the atoning blood of Jesus Christ, the Resurrection, and other cardinal principles of Scripture. Higher religious education brought a new enlightenment that in reality only challenged deeply rooted and long-held beliefs about God and eternity. Embracing the inerrancy of the Bible fell prey to philosophical reasoning, to scientific theories, and, eventually, to redefining biblical morality.

The question is, "How long will denominations once considered conservative hold out against the growing tide of modern and postmodern thought within their ranks?"

Under no circumstances should conservative believers be deceived into thinking that only mainline denominations are at risk. Every Christian church either has, or will, face the encroachment of liberal ideas about the Bible. Not one denomination is exempt—not the Baptists, the Lutherans, or the Pentecostals. These movements are confronting their own trials, often because of learning at a higher level—learning that frequently engenders questions about biblical interpretation and application.

Clearly, the history of religion in America is a record of diversity. Still, this nation began under the banner of renewed freedom in the Christian faith, and our early leaders saw the need to establish schools and colleges to support and propagate that faith. Over time, those leading institutions founded by the Episcopals, the Methodists, the Presbyterians, the Brethren, and others, began a long decline into liberal religious thought—a decline that oversaw the teaching and training of many ministers to think outside the Bible. One of the devastating consequences of such education has been the longtime questioning of the foundational doctrines of the New Testament.

What should our concerns be about the evangelical movement in the twenty-first century? Although many relatively conservative colleges and universities have flourished and have maintained some degree of scriptural balance, are they not susceptible to the same liberal religious thought that captured the mainline institutions? In fact, they are. The encroachment of biblical error into a church's teachings does not usually come in like a flood. Rather, the intrusion is subtle, almost imperceptible at first. Incrementally, educators adjust truth to better fit the culture, to have perhaps broader appeal, or, in some cases, simply to reduce accountability.

There is an undeniable tendency for more highly educated people to feel a greater sense of self-sufficiency and to experience a higher degree of human pride. Although it does not have to be this way, the inclination is certainly stronger. The knowledge the apostle Paul gained through the abundance of revelations given him by God brought with it a temptation for him to become arrogant. After God caught him up to the third heaven (see 2 Cor. 12:1-4), he wrote:

> For though I might desire to boast, I will not be a fool; for I will speak the truth. But I refrain, lest anyone should think of me above what he sees me to be or hears from me. And lest I should be exalted above measure by the abundance of the revelations, a thorn in the flesh was given to me, a

messenger of Satan to buffet me, lest I be exalted above measure (vv. 6-7).

This Scripture passage alone should give us pause. Considering how Satan tried to use Paul's own ego against him lets us know that we must, at all costs, guard against what Solomon referred to as "the little foxes that spoil the vines" (Song 2:15)—a reference to the small jackals in Israel that could destroy an entire vineyard by pulling on the vines, as these seeming harmless creatures feasted on the ripened grapes. The insidious encroachment of biblical error happens gradually. The very subtlety of it makes it extremely dangerous.

Just because something sounds good, just because someone we trust and like said it, and just because it seems to connect us more with our present culture does not make it acceptable. And just because a highly enlightened and well-respected college professor compellingly states a biblical proposition does not determine the validity of such a proposition. We have the daunting responsibility to evaluate every sermon, every lecture, and every conversation in the light of God's revealed Word. All that we learn in a lifetime, we must measure wisely against what "Thus says the Lord." For higher education to bring the anticipated benefits, it must always support biblical truth. Any deviation from that, however subtle or egregious, will only bring disappointment, frustration, and ultimate judgment.

There can be little doubt that the liberalizing of Christian churches begins in their institutions of higher learning.

Although that should not cause us to abandon our colleges and seminaries, it most definitely should cause us to reexamine our position on the cardinal doctrines of Scripture. Furthermore, it should lead evangelical bodies to spend more time in their conferences and assemblies prayerfully searching the Scriptures together, while humbly trembling before the Almighty in order to rightly divide and interpret God's Word.

Seminaries and church movements may change their doctrines, their interests, and their priorities. They may think outside the Bible for the sake of favorability, for the sake of financial support, or for the sake of less accountability to God. Yet, the Lord of the Church does not accommodate such changes, whatever the motives. In Him, "there is no variation or shadow of turning" (James 1:17). God, as truth, has established truth for time and eternity. The final authority is not man's interpretation of truth; it is God's meaning of truth. The responsibility rests on man to conform his interpretation to God's meaning through prayerful and sincere truth-seeking, through personal relationship building with Jesus Christ, and through cultivating a burning desire to honor Him in all things.

Again, pursuing higher education is a noble objective. Ministers and Christian workers need in-depth training in Bible doctrine and in the practical application of biblical principles. However, no level of formal education rises above the truth revealed in Jesus Christ. If religious education continues to serve the Christian movement by reinforcing the tenets of the Christian faith, it must always subordinate itself to this one glorious truth: "For God so loved the world that He gave His only begotten Son, that whoever believes in Him should not perish but have everlasting life" (John 3:16).

All that we believe about the Bible must fall under the umbrella of this all-encompassing truth—that God so loved the world that He gave His Son Jesus to die for our sins. If religious education divorces itself from this reality—the fact that no one can access God except through Jesus Christ—it can no longer remain a viable spiritual force in the world today.

10

⤬

Truth Dependent
on Legislative Process

"Go therefore and make disciples of all the nations, baptizing them in the name of the Father and of the Son and of the Holy Spirit" (Matt. 28:19).

In 1999, popular syndicated columnist Cal Thomas along with Ed Dobson, a former executive of the Moral Majority movement, coauthored the book *Blinded by Might*, a discussion of why the movement failed to accomplish its goals despite two decades of aggressive political maneuvering. Ultimately, both concluded that the Moral Majority, and all such Christian organizations, could never effect spiritual change through the political process, but only through fulfilling the Great Commission.[1]

For years now, evangelical Christians have worked hard to see born-again believers elected to political offices, confident that Christian influence in politics would make a significant difference in legislation. Unfortunately, the harsh political arena usually has a corrupting influence on well-meaning Christians who are intent on changing the system. For born-again politicians who have stood firm on biblical principles, their lasting effect on a system growing increasingly corrupt, and on the American public, has been negligible.

Should we give up on voting people of faith into political office? Certainly not. We desperately need Christians serving our nation in every possible way. What we cannot expect, however, is for believers to make earthshaking changes through the political process. Chances are, less-principled leaders who embrace the philosophy that the end always justifies the means will outmaneuver them at every turn.

The question we have to ask is this: "How did the Christian movement get to the place where it felt it had to resort to involvement in the political arena and in the legislative process to effect constructive change in our nation? Another question to consider is this: Where in the Scriptures does God tell us to build His kingdom through lawmaking and governmental regulation?

Christ gave only one commission to the church, and in that commission He declared, "Go into all the world and preach the gospel to every creature" (Mark 16:15). Nothing else we do will ever be as effective as this. The very purpose for the church remaining on the earth is to preach "Jesus Christ and Him crucified" (1 Cor. 2:2).

Surely, Satan must revel in knowing that the declining spiritual condition in the church has led the Christian movement in America to being reduced to little more than a political and social force. The church's depending on the legislative process to achieve her goals is a contradiction of disastrous proportions. Under no circumstances will the church ever win this war against spiritual wickedness in high places, against powers and principalities (see Eph. 6:12), through political bargaining and maneuvering.

Again, I do not disparage Christians from running for political office. On the contrary, I rejoice that more people who represent my religious beliefs have committed to public service. Christian influence in virtually every area of our society can only be good, and that most certainly includes government and politics. As with tradition, philosophy, marketing strategies, and higher education, the biggest concern is subordination to biblical truth.

In the past fifty years or so, the church in America has grossly misinterpreted God's instructions, thinking that perhaps its greatest contribution to the well-being of our society comes by tackling social issues through education, psychology, technology, and political strategizing. Again, the problem is not as much about utilizing these means but, rather, the church's major emphasis shifting to ancillary matters. The Christian movement's time and energies overly expended for causes other than fulfilling the Great Commission only takes it out of its game plan.

Basically, the church has moved from being a powerful offensive force to effect spiritual change to scarcely clinging to a defensive position, simply hoping not to lose ground. How did it happen? How is it that the church bought into the social agenda as her first priority?

Having first seen the light of day on January 5, 1950, I have vivid recollections of the late '50s and '60s. Being a student of history, I also have a reasonable understanding of the strengths and challenges of America leading into the middle of the twentieth century. For example, during and following World War II, our nation experienced a period of remarkable economic growth and material prosperity. New technology opened the door to a promising future. The American family was still strong, unemployment was low, and dreams of a peaceful coexistence with all the peoples of the world abounded.

Somewhere in the midst of material prosperity, and maybe because of it, undesirable elements began to appear with considerable frequency. Americans began to drop out of church, and family life started deteriorating. The nation witnessed the beginning of the drug epidemic, while the Supreme Court announced in 1963 that no longer was it legal to read the Bible and pray in our public schools. Rebellion among America's youth became commonplace as riots broke out on college campuses. Teenagers, empty because of their parents' materialistic preoccupations, ran away from home to escape the superficiality of the establishment.

I do not believe that a single decision by our highest court started our headlong plunge into secularism and moral degeneracy. The problem ran much deeper than merely canceling a three-minute devotional each morning in our school classrooms. The ban on prayer and Bible reading, though a grave injustice, did not appreciably alter Christian education in this nation. Rather, it was symptomatic of a growing undercurrent of humanistic philosophy pervading not only our educational system, but also virtually every secular institution in existence, as well as some religious institutions.

During this calamitous culture shift, absolutes slowly faded into oblivion, blurring the line between right and wrong. The Ten Commandments, which had served as the guideline for moral behavior for more than three thousand years, became grossly distorted. America lost her moral compass and has never since been the same.

The questions remain, "How did we get here, and what role has the church played in the process?" Instead of pointing a finger of accusation at the Supreme Court, the government, the secular humanists, the anti-Christian crusaders, and spineless politicians, the church has to point the finger back to itself. Perhaps the better question is, "How did the Christian movement in America allow the religious, social, and political landscapes to decline so drastically?"

We have to face the harsh reality that the social, educational, and political systems in our nation are not as responsible for the decline of the Christian movement as much as the church is responsible for the progressive decay in our secular institutions. Somewhere in the past, we began playing defense. The church relinquished her position as the voice of morality and evangelism and resorted to sounding the trumpet for social change. Even though many of these changes have been needed, the church made the mistake of tackling these issues through the application of sociological and psychological principles, often at the expense of sound scriptural principles.

Like many people, I have always enjoyed a variety of sports. Some I have played, while others I have only watched. One particular sport I have thoroughly enjoyed through the years is racquetball. I always found that it provided a good workout—about as close to aerobics as I care to get—and allowed for good interaction with a friendly opponent (I never really cared about playing with an unfriendly one). Because I never took lessons, it took me a while to learn strategy—probably because most opponents were not teachers, and even if they were, they never wanted to give a challenger any pointers on how to win.

During the mid-1980s, a young man from Lee College in Cleveland, Tennessee (now Lee University), came to work with me in a pastorate in Denver, Colorado. Mark was athletic, full of energy, and immediately began playing on our church softball team. I soon discovered that he also played racquetball, leading me to set an appointment for him to join me on the racquetball court. I should have known better . . . me being in my mid-thirties and him being college-age.

Although I had considered myself a decent player and had competed against some fairly good athletes, Mark consistently played a better game than anyone else I had played against. He had a good backhand, a devastating forehand,

and always seemed to be in good position. After losing my first three or four matches against him, I knew something had to change if I continued to enjoy this game, especially against one of my staff members.

Following one of those matches, I sat silent in the driver's seat of my car waiting to start the engine, with Mark sitting silent beside me in the passenger's seat. Without emotion, and without looking in his direction, I simply announced, "I am *going* to beat you." The spirit of competition overwhelmed me at that moment, and I simply could not help myself. Just saying it made me feel better.

I will never forget Mark's quick and unassertive response. He simply answered, "You'll have to get me out of the middle." This young, just-out-of-college, youth pastor of mine taught me more about racquetball that day than anyone had in a long time. His simple answer occupied my mind constantly until our next game. Amazingly, his nine words revealed weaknesses in my game I had not been able to identify before. The more I thought about what he said, the better I developed my strategy for our next competition. From that point on, I began to win some matches. He was younger and stronger than I was, and my forehand never matched his; but I learned to play position in a way I never had before, and that made a remarkable difference.

To be successful in racquetball competition, a player needs to control center court, and control it without fear of being struck in the back or in the back of the head with the ball. Otherwise, he could quickly find himself with his back literally "against the wall." With the whole court open, the opponent has an easy "kill shot."

What the church in America has slowly done over the past fifty or more years is to give up "center court." We have lost our position of spiritual influence; we have our backs against the wall and seem to be barely hanging on in a defensive mode. Having given up passionately proclaiming the gospel of Jesus Christ as the only way of salvation, the church has been reduced to battling for the minds of people through relevancy, through carnal campaigns, and through the legislative process.

The very thing that works best is the very thing we have pushed into the background—winning souls. Nothing has the power to change a person or a nation like God's Word does. With all the destructive forces working inside the Roman Empire to bring about its collapse, probably nothing contributed to that collapse more than the spread of Christianity.

The New Testament church visibly burst on the scene in Acts 2 and immediately began to expand throughout Jerusalem, Judea, Samaria, and beyond. The fledgling church had received a mandate from Christ and passionately sought to fulfill it. Interestingly, this remarkable expansion of Christianity happened under the noses of some of Rome's most corrupt emperors, and under the oppressive Roman regime they superintended.

Nowhere in the writings of Paul, Peter, James, and John do we find any instructions to resist governments, or even to change governments, in an effort to enforce a nation's compliance with biblical principles. They understood that the expansion of Christianity would not come through the legislative process. On the other hand, at least two of these apostles, Paul and Peter, cautioned believers against disrespecting governments and political leaders:

> Let every soul be subject to the governing authorities. For there is no authority except from God, and the authorities that exist are appointed by God. Therefore, whoever resists the authority resists the ordinance of God, and those who resist will bring judgment on themselves. For rulers are not a terror to good works, but to evil. . . . Do what is good, and you will have praise from the same (Rom. 13:1-3).

> Therefore submit yourselves to every ordinance of man for the Lord's sake, whether to the king as supreme, or to governors, as to those who are sent by him for the punishment of evildoers and for the praise of those who do good. For this is the will of God, that by doing good you may put to silence the ignorance of foolish men—as free, yet not using liberty as a cloak for vice, but as bondservants of God. Honor all people. Love the brotherhood. Fear God. Honor the king (1 Peter 2:13-17).

If these two most noted apostles felt compelled to challenge the followers of Christ to submit to Rome's civil authority, then where should we bring our focus to bear today in a nation not yet closely resembling the repressive nature of the Roman Empire?

The best way to change the conscience of a nation is not through the election process, not through appointing (in the case of the United States) conservative Supreme Court justices, and not through writing new laws. The best way—in fact, the only way—is to experience a spiritual awakening to the point where the church once again does what Christ called it to do, which is to spread the good news of God's plan of salvation in an effort to lead a nation's people to the Cross.

Granted, the church cannot force Christianity upon anyone, nor has it been very effective in the past decades in *leading* people to Christ. Sadly, during the latter half of the twentieth century and the beginning of the new one, the church in America seems to have lost its passion and vision for the harvest.

If the church is to reclaim her rightful position in America, she cannot wait for government to hand it back to her, because that will never happen. The church can only reclaim "center court" through prayer and fasting, through applying biblical principles to daily life, and by once again fulfilling the Great Commission—"Go into all the world and preach the gospel. . . ." The spread of truth cannot depend on legislation. If the church waits for government to enforce her rights, the truth will never get beyond our own walls.

Will a spiritual awakening in the church greatly shake a nation such as ours, one that has drifted so far from truth? No one knows for sure. Spiritual renewal always has a positive effect on people, but only God knows how much of an influence it would now have on America. However, the words of the prophet Joel should encourage us: "Who knows if He will turn and relent, and leave a blessing behind Him?" (2:14).

11

⁓⊱⊰⁓

Truth Recovered

Now when they brought out the money that was brought into the house of the Lord, Hilkiah the priest found the Book of the Law of the Lord given by Moses. Then Hilkiah answered and said to Shaphan the scribe, "I have found the Book of the Law in the house of the Lord" (2 Chron. 34:14-15).

God's Word lost in His own house! How could that be? How could King Josiah, his predecessors, along with the priests and leaders in Judah, allow that to happen? As inconceivable as it is that the Jewish people lost the Law of God in the Temple, it is even more alarming that no one missed it—not the king, not the priests, and not the people.

Similarly, it is troubling that in today's religious climate, *truth* has become a casualty. It is just as troubling, if not more so, that few professing believers seem to miss it. When truth is discarded, dismissed, or carelessly lost in the church itself and no one seems to notice, the "handwriting" is about to appear on "the wall"—God's handwriting that spells divine retribution, either to call professing believers to repentance through chastisement, or to cut off for good those who only outwardly profess faith in Christ. Handling the truth dismissively or carelessly always brings devastating consequences.

We left King Josiah, in chapter 2, bringing reformation to Judah. He approached his task with vigor, doing all in his power as king to rid Judah of idolatry. In 2 Chronicles 34:8, after Josiah had purged the land of its groves and idols, he sent Shaphan the scribe, Maaseiah the governor of the city, and Joah the recorder to repair the house of the Lord. They delivered money appropriated for these repairs into the hands of the high priest, Hilkiah, who in turn put it into the hands of the artisans and builders.

In the process of repairing the Temple, Hilkiah made a remarkable discovery. Verses 14-18 record this amazing finding:

> Now when they brought out the money that was brought into the house of the Lord, Hilkiah the priest found the Book of the Law of the Lord given by Moses. Then Hilkiah answered and said to Shaphan the scribe, "I have found the Book of the Law in the house of the Lord." And Hilkiah gave the book to Shaphan. So Shaphan carried the book to the king. . . . Then Shaphan the scribe told the king, saying, "Hilkiah the priest has given me a book." And Shaphan read it before the king.

As effective as Josiah's reformations had been, the finding of the Book of the Law marked a turning point for him and all Judah. Up until now, all that he had done, he had done more or less on his own. His efforts had not significantly affected the conscience of the nation, and not much enthusiasm had followed the new reforms.[1]

No doubt, Shaphan, like Hilkiah, became so moved by the discovery of the Book of the Law in the Temple, and by his understanding of what had been written therein, that he could hardly wait to bring it to the king. Upon entering the king's chambers, he gave a report of the disbursing of building-fund money to the workers, assuring him that they were doing their work. Following his report on the Temple repairs, he announced that Hilkiah had given him a book. Without fanfare or commentary, he began to read, letting the words from the Book of the Law speak for themselves.

With Shaphan's reading of the Book of the Law to the king, reality began to settle in—the reality that the statutes God had given to His people to keep had been shamefully neglected. The king, the priests and scribes, as well as other officials of the court, had neglected them.

Shaphan's reading of the selected portions of the Book of the Law smote the heart of the king. In contrition, Josiah took hold of his clothes and tore them, expressing his grief that he and Judah's leaders had neglected God's law. He immediately commanded Hilkiah, Ahikam, Abdon, and Shaphan to inquire of the Lord concerning the words of the book that Hilkiah had just found. He cried, "For great is the wrath of the Lord that is poured out on us, because our fathers have not kept the word of the Lord, to do according to all that is written in this book" (v. 21).

The men appointed by the king consulted Huldah the prophetess, a prominent woman and the wife of Shallum, the keeper of the wardrobe. Unhesitatingly, she spoke piercing words that revealed the judgment of God upon Judah for their idolatry. Concerning Josiah, she declared, "Because your heart was tender, and you humbled yourself before God when you heard His words against this place . . . I will gather you to your fathers, and you shall be gathered to your grave in peace" (vv. 27-28).

In response to the words of the Lord, Josiah renewed his efforts in bringing reformation. He assembled the elders of Judah and Jerusalem, the priests, prophets, and all the people before the house of the Lord to hear the words of the Book of the Law read again. As he stood by one of the pillars of the Temple, he led the people in making "a covenant before the Lord, to follow the Lord and to keep His commandments and His testimonies and His statutes, with all his heart and all his soul, to perform the words of this covenant that were written in this book" (2 Kings 23:3).

It is important to note that Josiah, as the head of all Judah and Jerusalem, led the way in renewal by rededicating himself to God and truth. If "judgment [must] begin at the house of God" (1 Peter 4:17), it follows that leaders entrusted with the spiritual well-being of a people are the ones to lead the way.

Although Josiah had already accomplished much in bringing Judah back to the one true God, he now stepped up the pace in reforming this land that had become woefully immersed in idolatry. Not only did he intensify his labors to destroy all the visible idols inside and outside the Temple, he now brought his attention to bear on the dry bones of the prophets of Baal and Ashtoreth buried in the ground out of sight.

God now moves Josiah to do more than deal with the visible corruptions in the land. Genuine reformation must go beyond addressing immoral behavior externally. It must penetrate deep below the surface, "even to the division of soul and spirit, and of joints and marrow" (Heb. 4:12). Since external appearance and conduct are only symptomatic of what lies deep in the heart, sincere renewal and commitment will never occur unless truth reaches man's innermost being.

After true repentance and rededication, the king began to see what could not literally be seen—the pollution lying beneath the surface. "As Josiah turned, he saw the tombs that were there on the mountain. And he sent and took the bones out of the tombs and burned them on the altar, and defiled it according to the word of the Lord which the man of God proclaimed" (2 Kings 23:16).

With renewed vigor, Josiah had the bones of the false prophets and priests, who had so vilely corrupted Judah and had suppressed its expressions of the true worship of Jehovah, dug up and burned on the altar of God. He would not rest until he had done all he could to bring Judah back to the God of Abraham, Isaac, and Jacob. Partial reformation is no reformation at all. Unless rededication to God is full and complete, nothing much has changed.

The kind of change needed in the church today, in the lives of professing believers, is a change that only God's Word can bring to pass. It will not come through a simple desire to conform to the behavior and practices of the surrounding religious culture. It will only come through pure motives, through rediscovering God's Word. Until there is a rediscovery of truth, reforms will only be superficial. On the other hand, finding again the Book of Truth will always influence lives for the good. The Word of Truth at work reveals sin, brings conviction, effects repentance, and leads to godly actions.

For decades in America, layers of traditions, philosophies, and secular strategies covered biblical truth. Sadly, the professing Christian church has perpetuated these ideas. Therefore, if truth has been lost to our culture, it happened because it first became lost in the church. Lying somewhere in an unlit back room and covered with a thick layer of dust, truth has languished, out of sight and out of mind, and was replaced by man's grossly limited knowledge, worldly wisdom, and human ingenuity.

Considering the times in which we live, and the evidence of the soon return of Christ, now is surely the time to rediscover truth (the Word of God), brush the dust from it, open it, read it, hide it in our hearts, and put it once again into practice. The spiritual life of professing believers depends on it; the spiritual life and effectiveness of the Christian movement depend on it; the healing of our nation depends on it.

In the heart of every rational person rests an overwhelming desire for freedom—freedom from fear, bondage, and oppression; and, whether everyone realizes it or not, freedom from guilt and sin. This freedom, though, only comes through truth; truth sets us free. However, unless we recover and hold fast to truth, not only do believers stand to lose, but the entire unbelieving populace of a nation will lose, not having the privilege of hearing the gospel of Jesus Christ in unadulterated form.

Paul underscored the power and benefit of truth: "Therefore take up the whole armor of God, that you may be able to withstand in the evil day, and having done all, to stand. Stand therefore, having girded your waist with truth" (Eph. 6:13-14).

Truth is not only our guide into all that is pure and right, it is also our protection. Truth is cleansing, instructive, empowering, and wonderfully liberating. If we can once again embrace truth in its entirety and, with the psalmist David, "hide it in our hearts" (see 119:11), the recovered and applied truth revealed in Jesus will not only change us, but will potentially change our surroundings and, yes, even our nation!

12

❦❧

Truth: The Only Hope

*For whatever things were written before were written
for our learning, that we through patience and comfort of
the Scriptures might have hope* (Rom. 15:4).

Truth is the only hope of man. Empires rise and fall, ideas germinate and die, systems develop and dissolve, and styles appear and disappear. But truth is that one unshakable foundation, established in the heavens.

Although all the kingdoms of this world are destined to pass away, Christ's kingdom will stand forever. Even though systems of philosophy will cease to exist, the truth embodied in Jesus Christ endures; denominations will disappear, but the true Church will continue; creeds decay and wax old, but the Bible possesses an indestructible energy; the heavens and the earth shall pass away, but God's Word abides forever.

Truth has almost imperceptibly slipped away from many believers, only to be replaced by tradition, position, marketing strategies, liberal religious education, human philosophy, and a quest for self-fulfillment. But truth can still be found once again—by turning the pages of the Bible and prayerfully poring over its contents.

In the Scriptures alone, we have hope. The valid expectation of a better day ahead does not come through governments, political leaders, military forces, nor even religious leaders and institutions. This hope only comes through the manifestation of God's Son. Perhaps the single most profound witness to the truthfulness of God's Word is the bodily resurrection of Jesus Christ.

One particular evening some years ago—when our oldest son, Scott, was about four years old and our youngest, Shane, was still an infant—while sitting at the dinner table, I carefully explained to Scott the meanings of the words *faith, hope,* and *love.* In particular, I stressed the word *hope,* knowing that in the scriptural sense it was often more difficult to define. I really felt like the wise father, instilling a deep spiritual truth in the heart of my child—a truth that I was sure he would immediately grasp for time and eternity.

The next evening, again sitting at the dinner table, I decided to quiz him on our Bible discussion from the previous evening.

"Scott," I asked, "could you tell your mother and me what the word *hope* means?"

"Yes sir, I think I can," he responded. In between noisy bites of food, he slowly and thoughtfully explained, "If me . . . and Mother . . . and Shane were gone, and you were here in the house all by yourself, if somebody broke in, you *hope* they don't kill you!"

I quickly responded, "You've got that right!" Although I had not anticipated that explanation, I quickly had to agree with his sincere childlike assessment—an assessment that had more to do with wishful thinking than with comprehending the mystical resurrection and eternal existence of the believer.

Conversely, *hope* in the spiritual sense is much more than wishful thinking. The Greek word is *elpis,* which means "favorable and confident expectation." In fact, *hope* is the first development of *faith*. It is the fertile ground upon which faith grows. Hope is able to calm a soul that is troubled and to cheer a despondent heart. It looks with joyful anticipation to the glory that is to come. It reaches beyond the visible, the tangible, and the audible, and has the same object as that of our faith, Jesus Christ.

In February 2007, Oscar-winning director, James Cameron (*Titanic*), along with an Emmy award-winning documentary filmmaker, held a press conference in New York to promote a film they had produced for the Discovery Channel, titled *The Lost Tomb of Jesus.* They displayed some bone boxes discovered in Jerusalem in 1980, claiming that the boxes came from the "family tomb" of Jesus and that one of the boxes actually contained the remains of Jesus.

Could any pastor imagine what preaching an Easter sermon would be like if that particular bone box indeed contained the bones of Jesus Christ? Consider what that would be like. It would sound something like this:

> We have just received word that the bones of Jesus Christ have been found in a tomb in Jerusalem. To be quite honest

with you, I have struggled with this news more than I have ever struggled with anything. Let's face it—it is hard for us to believe. It just does not seem possible.

I have found myself reflecting on my past and on what I considered my rich Christian heritage—that is, growing up in a strong Christian family and attending Sunday school and church all my life. As a young teenager, I believed God called me into the ministry. I have spent my entire life believing in the power of prayer. Likewise, I have spent my ministry counseling people to trust this Book—the Bible. I have preached that God forgives, restores, heals, delivers, and offers eternal life.

In the past few days, however, we have heard disturbing news—news that Jesus is still dead. I do not know anything more earthshaking than that. I would have prepared an Easter sermon to preach to you, but there is no need for that now. It would not really make any difference.

The fact is, we have come to the end of a journey—a journey that has turned out to be empty and meaningless. There is no need to continue. As much as I hate to admit it, it is all over. We have been wrong, and that is hard to accept.

The revelation that the remains of Jesus have been found means you are still in your sins. In addition, the faith you thought you had was not real after all. Your faith has been in vain. Not only has your faith been in vain, my preaching has also been in vain. Everything we have done in relationship to Christ has been nothing more than an exercise in futility.

As your pastor, I have to inform you that there will be no more church services or Bible studies here. We will be closing the doors for good next week. And that means I will no longer have a job, and you will no longer need a place of worship. I had believed so strongly that Jesus was the Christ, the Messiah. My entire life, I have built on the belief that Jesus rose from the dead, and that He would come again. Unfortunately, that appears now to have been in vain.

I know we all love to fellowship together. And we can still do that—have a meal at someone's home and share together. But even that won't be the same. We all know that our fellowship has been enhanced because we believed we were part of the same body of Christ. But that now seemingly has changed.

I would end my message with an altar call, but there is no use; it would only be a waste of time. Or, I could simply close with prayer, but that, too, would be meaningless. I suppose I could simply wish you well and dismiss you. Yet, if Christ is dead, you will be facing a harsh and hostile world without any divine help.

In closing, I guess all I can really say to you is, just make it the best way you can. Considering that the recently discovered bones of Jesus leave us with absolutely no hope, I do not suppose any of us can make it at all. For that, I am truly sorry. Since we no longer have hope in Christ, all we can really expect is to live our lives out in sheer misery.

Could any message be more disheartening and depressing? Certainly not. Yet, that is the message Paul gives the church in Corinth in 1 Corinthians 15:12-19:

> Now if Christ be preached that he rose from the dead, how say some among you that there is no resurrection of the

dead? But if there be no resurrection of the dead, then is Christ not risen: And if Christ be not risen, then is our preaching vain, and your faith is also vain. Yea, and we are found false witnesses of God; because we have testified of God that he raised up Christ: whom he raised not up, if so be that the dead rise not. For if the dead rise not, then is not Christ raised: And if Christ be not raised, your faith is vain; ye are yet in your sins. Then they also which are fallen asleep in Christ are perished. If in this life only we have hope in Christ, we are of all men most miserable (KJV).

Thankfully, Paul didn't end his correspondence with these words. If he had, we would indeed be "of all men most miserable," helpless and hopeless.

After discussing the despair that the lifeless body of Jesus Christ would bring, Paul continued, expressing the truth that has stood the test of times and, in the face of biblical distortions and compromise, continues to give hope to all who dare trust in Him and abide in His Word:

But now Christ is risen from the dead, and has become the firstfruits of those who have fallen asleep. For since by man came death, by Man also came the resurrection of the dead. For as in Adam all die, even so in Christ all shall be made alive (vv. 20-22).

In reality, the discovery of these interesting bones in 1980 in Jerusalem, by construction workers digging a foundation for a new building, had nothing to do with the death of Jesus. These bones only proved what we already knew—that is, the name *Jesus* was so common two thousand years ago that it appears on many other tombs and many other bone boxes.

We also know something else. The bones of Jesus will never be found because He is not here; He has risen! The record of His resurrection is clear. Hundreds of witnesses saw Him after His crucifixion. And being convinced of His crucifixion, His resurrection, and His ascension, assures us that He is coming again!

Several years ago, when Sandra and I made our second trip together to Israel, I remember standing before Gordon's Tomb on a beautiful Sunday morning. The sun brightly streamed through the gnarled olive trees, highlighting the fragrant flowers and greenery within this tranquil garden. Before us lay the empty tomb believed by many to have been the actual burial tomb of Jesus.

As we stood together with our group pondering the possible implications of this small piece of real estate, a young Baptist minister from England—one who served on staff for the site—respectfully walked near the entrance to this old burial tomb. Lifting his voice and gesturing with his hands, he began to speak, the tenor of his voice rising and falling with each new emotion.

I shall never forget his brief yet poignant discourse, which he concluded with these thoughts: "If the world wants to destroy Christianity, it doesn't have to publicly curse us, malign us in the newspapers, slander us through various other media, or attack us physically. If the world really wants to destroy Christianity, let them give us the body of Jesus Christ."

Briefly pausing for effect, the young minister thoughtfully turned toward the tomb behind him—a tomb whose stone had been long since rolled away, and which invited visitors an inquisitive look inside. Now having everyone's eyes and ears, he lifted his left hand toward the tomb and victoriously announced, "But He is not here . . . the tomb is empty! The body of Jesus will never be given to us because He is not dead—He is alive!"

Spiritual hope is not rooted in political systems, social evolution, or in charismatic leaders. No one will find it in the traditions of man, in elevation to high office, in human strategy, in formal education, in philosophy, or in material wealth. Spiritual hope rests only on the solid foundation of truth, God's unshakable truth. It is the truth that God exists and that He prepared the way for Christ to come to earth to die for us—the truth that Jesus rose from the dead and is now seated at the right hand of the Father, making intercessions for us, and is destined to return in clouds of great power and glory to judge the unfaithful and to reward the righteous.

This is the only truth. Anything added to, or taken away from, this established Word of God is in error and its purveyors are subject to divine retribution (Deut. 4:2; Rev. 22:18-19).

On the other hand, Jesus promised freedom to those who abide in truth—freedom from sin, from fear, from divine retribution, and, ultimately, from mortality. And this is where we find spiritual hope—in the assurance of a bodily resurrection: "a building from God, a house not made with hands, eternal in the heavens" (2 Cor. 5:1).

The bodily resurrection of Jesus Christ is the validation of truth; therefore, it is the assurance that just as He rose from the dead and lives forever, we shall also rise again and live forever in His presence. The apostle John declared: "Beloved, now we are children of God; and it has not yet been revealed what we shall be, but we know that when He is revealed, we shall be like Him, for we shall see Him as He is. And everyone who has this hope in Him purifies himself, just as He is pure" (1 John 3:2-3).

❦

Epilogue

What makes accepting *truth* so difficult? Why is there the predisposition to twist it, adjust it, modify it, or simply deny it? From the beginning of time, it has been that way—from the time that Eve fell into the serpent's trap and began to rationalize changing God's instructions for a perceived personal benefit.

In the broader sense, the answer is *sin*. The sinful condition of man, which is set against the righteous nature of God, naturally recoils at truth and obedience. In the specific sense, corrupt man simply does not want to be held responsible and accountable, and truth does both.

Just as truth is demanding, not leaving any room for departure from it, it is also liberating, leaving much room for living life in joyful anticipation of the perfect future. "Then Jesus said to those Jews who believed Him, 'If you abide in My word, you are My disciples indeed. And you shall know the truth, and the truth shall make you free'" (John 8:31-32). Truth is the only fully liberating force in life.

For example, genuine freedom for people within a given nation does not come through the exercise of force. That is, it does not come through military power, political strategies, or economic sanctions, because true freedom is more than protection from a visible enemy, more than the promises of a government, and more than the pursuit of happiness. The show of force or the employment of social strategies, however well intended, does not liberate humanity from bondage to sin, or from bondage to the guilt and fear associated with sin.

Only through knowing *the* truth, and through truth's application, is there liberation. There are many truths known by man—the laws of nature, irrefutable scientific properties, hard-and-fast mathematical formulas, and other constants. These are God's established truths, but not *the* truth. The *truth* discussed in the previous chapters is the marvelous truth of man's redemption through Jesus Christ. Without this truth, man remains in bondage with no hope of freedom.

Jesus made it clear that man had to *know* the truth. Truth can only become personal and life-changing if it is first known. Knowing the seasons of nature, understanding molecular composition, and comprehending the laws of mathematics have no power to change lives internally. Although these truths serve us well, alone they have no effect on the sin nature of man. Knowledge of *the* truth is the highest attainable knowledge, and, consequently, is the only truth able to deal with man's corrupt nature.

Only when a person knows the truth of redemption manifested in Christ—forgiveness, justification, and reconciliation through faith—can that person begin to apprehend, or experience, the blessing of spiritual freedom.[1] Paul understood this when he cried out, "That I may know Him . . ." (Phil. 3:10)—that is, to intimately know Christ.

No wonder Satan attacks *the* truth so viciously. He knows that if man distorts, compromises, or changes the truth revealed in Jesus Christ in any way, then his opportunity for eternal freedom vanishes. Man continues to live in slavery, in guilt, and in fear of judgment.

To prepare His disciples for His return, and to prepare believers of every generation for this event, Jesus first warned about deception: "Take heed that no one deceives you. For many will come in My name, saying, 'I am the Christ,' and will deceive many" (Matt. 24:4-5). He knew the greatest challenge for His followers in the last days would be truth watered down, adjusted to suit man's carnal desires. Christ understood that Satan would keep his sights set on Christianity and would use (more effectively) deception as his ammunition.

The assurance we have is that *the* truth is still liberating. If we tenaciously cling to it, it will never fail us. The world around us may be shaking uncontrollably, and the whole creation may be groaning and travailing (Rom. 8:22), but we know that through Jesus Christ the Truth, we are "more than conquerors . . . and shall never be separated from the love of God" (see vv. 37-39).

The author of Hebrews (perhaps Paul) issued this warning:

See that you do not refuse Him who speaks. For if they did not escape who refused Him who spoke on earth, much more shall we not escape if we turn away from Him who speaks from heaven, whose voice then shook the earth; but now He has promised, saying, "Yet once more I shake not only the earth, but also heaven." Now this, "Yet once more," indicates the removal of those things that are being shaken, as of things that are made, that the things which cannot be shaken may remain (12:25-27).

After the mighty schemes of man dissipate, after the kingdoms of this world crumble to the ground, and after the heavens and earth in their present forms "pass away with a great noise, and the elements will melt with fervent heat" (2 Peter 3:10), the one thing that will remain is *truth*. This means the truth of God, His throne, His Son and Savior, His Holy Spirit, and His Church—and with that, life everlasting.

❦❦

Endnotes

Chapter 2

[1] "The Book of Second Kings," *The Pulpit Commentary* (Grand Rapids: Eerdmans, 1950) 442.

[2] "The Book of Second Kings," 441.

Chapter 3

[1] "The Book of First Samuel," *The Pulpit Commentary* (Grand Rapids: Eerdmans, 1950) 95.

Chapter 4

[1] Bertrand Russell, *A History of Western Philosophy* (New York: Simon and Schuster, 1945) 13.

[2] Michael Murray and Michael Rea, "Philosophy and Christian Theology," *The Stanford Encyclopedia of Philosophy* (Fall 2012), ed. Edward N. Zalta, *plato.stanford,edu/archives/fall2012/entries/christian-theology-philosophy.*

[3] Ralph McInerny and John Callaghan, "Saint Thomas Aquinas," *The Stanford Encyclopedia of Philosophy* (Winter 2010), ed. Edward N. Zalta, *plato.stanford.edu/archives/win2010/entries/aquinas.*

[4] "The Book of Colossians," *The Pulpit Commentary,* 111.

Chapter 6

[1] "The Book of Psalms," *The Pulpit Commentary* (Grand Rapids: Eerdmans) 289.

[2] "The Book of Exodus," *The Pulpit Commentary,* 165.

Chapter 9

[1] Mitchell Landsberg, "Claremont Seminary Reaches Beyond Christianity," *Los Angeles Times*, June 9, 2010.

[2] Grant Wacker, "Religious Liberalism and the Modern Crisis of Faith," *nationalhumanitiescenter.org/tserve/divam.htm*.

Chapter 10

[1] Ed Dobson and Cal Thomas, *Blinded by Might* (Grand Rapids: Zondervan, 1999).

Chapter 11

[1] "The Book of Second Kings," *The Pulpit Commentary*, 449.

Epilogue

[1] "The Book of John," *The Pulpit Commentary*, 393.